AMERICA, THEIR AMERICA

America

THEIR AMERICA

J. P. CLARK

AFRICANA PUBLISHING CORPORATION · NEW YORK
An affiliate of International University Booksellers, Inc.

First published
in the United States of America 1969
by Africana Publishing Corporation
101 Fifth Avenue
New York, N.Y. 10003

Library of Congress catalog card no. 79—80851

First published by André Deutsch 1964
Reprinted 1971

For RUTH *and* SAM, CAT *and* ISRAEL,
NAOMI, GLORIA, NORMA *and* DICK
WATKINS *as well as* JAMES WARD, SAM
ALLEN, RUTH JETT *and others who gave me
backing even when the going seemed bad for
me in the United States, and who I know
will not ride this hobby-horse of mine down a
course or to posts I had at no time in mind*

Printed in Malta by
St Paul's Press Ltd

Contents

Foreword

JP, as the author of *America, Their America* is affectionately called by his close friends, is one of Nigeria's most versatile writers. The present book, *America, Their America*, undoubtedly establishes him as an able journalist, a keen social observer and critic.

I suspect the primary consideration for being asked to write an introduction to this edition is because, unlike JP who spent just about a year in the United States, I lived there for a little over a dozen years. Unlike JP, I was for some time a 'regular' student, and for a short period, a wage earner in the United States. In the circumstances, I was unable to avail myself of the broad sweeping experience which a well financed programme made possible for him. For example, he travelled more widely in the United States in so short a time than I did in more than a dozen years. There is no doubt that this gave him considerable advantage to observe the varieties of life in their America. To some extent prolonged stay had dulled my sensitivities to much that was going on around me. But *America, Their America* eloquently confirms much of my apprehension about many well-intentioned American programmes of student exchange. The revelations about the way in which the Central Intelligence Agency has exploited American philanthropic organisations in the interest of United States world-wide imperialism have confirmed my diffidence about student exchange programmes.

JP went to the States on a well financed, carefully planned exchange program intended to introduce him as well as other 'underdeveloped intellectuals' to what Americans believe to be the fortress of twentieth century democracy. Like all such programs designed for short-term visitors to the United States, the stage was well laid out, and the actors and actresses fully rehearsed. However, in spite of, or because of, all the efforts meant to make the 'guest feel at home', the whole show was spoilt by two factors: a bad stage manager and the inscrutable, unpredictable spectator. JP's account in this book of his experiences in the United States is note-worthy for his honesty and frankness.

For one who believes that international understanding, co-operation and friendship among peoples must be based on fair and honest dealings and on mutual respect, *America, Their America* is a most welcome book. It is an important commentary on contemporary American society, and especially on the massive efforts of the United States policy-makers to make friends and influence poeple abroad. This book should be read by Africans wishing to learn about America. Americans, too, should profit from it. If Americans would learn from what the author has to say, they would save themselves and others much unnecessary embarrassment. Were such the case, JP would be paying great tribute to the Parvin Program of Princeton University and to his American hosts.

Painfully struck by the continuing exploitation and oppression of black Americans, JP could not help admitt-ing to himself, as he 'entered the heart of the establishment, that America is a white country, with blacks merely there on terms worse than sufferance. For those who understand the profound tragedy of Americans of African descent in the United States, the fact that the 'Negro people will continue for several decades to occupy . . . the position of the unwanted child who, having been brought for a visit, must remain for the rest of his life', is not too harsh a conclusion. Moreover, America is not only a white man's country but also, according to the late American sociologist C. Wright Mills, a society dominated by a 'power elite', consisting of an interlocking directorate of the 'top brass' of the giant business corporations, the government, and the military. Lastly America is obsessed with sex.

But it is not these observations alone (even if we regard them as abstractions) which make the book important and interesting. Rather it is the author's ability to pierce through the fog of official propaganda and stage-management into the 'heart of the matter', and his reactions to America's cold war 'struggle for the minds of men' in Africa, Asia and Latin America.

JP does not theorise; instead he takes the reader through many varied situations which poignantly reveal 'their America'. The reader travels with the author to the scenes of his experiences. He moves from the 'holy recess and study' of Princeton University to the small town newspaper office, and from there to the mammoth *Washington Post* establishment; from professional gatherings and conferences with State Department officials to the Supreme Court of the United States; from Afro-American communities and organisations to private American homes. He meets African students, and ponders the consequences of uprooting youngsters from their countries for a prolonged period of study in the United States. He questions the effects on the development of African universities of siphoning off the most promising students for undergraduate courses in the United States. The author's reactions to these and other situations are fascinatingly recorded. No doubt, these reactions reveal as much about the American hosts as their maverick guest whose qualities of mental independence, sensitivity, and insight into men and matters are here in full play. The result is an illuminating book, written with superb clarity and spiced with touches of poetry.

It would be a mistake to attribute JP's reactions purely to personal idiosyncracies, for the problems he came up against transcend his personal dilemma. It is the problem of white America, deeply rooted in the American historical experience and ideology, and rendered even more pronounced today (and unbearable to the outsider) by the necessities of the cold war struggle for the minds of men. From its founding, Americans, especially Anglo-Americans, have thought of themselves as God's 'chosen people'. They feel that they have established for themselves a society, the like of which has never been known or may yet be the luck of any other nation. Because of this belief, they have sought to compel all other groups in the country to assimilate into the specifically Anglo-American 'ideal' of the good life or the good society. For Americans, writes, JP. 'revolution of any . . . type is a state and ideal already completely and permanently achieved at home by their founding and fighting fathers several centuries back.'

Because Americans believe theirs to be an approximation of the ideal society, they believe also that they have a mission to extend the benefit of their experience even to the most unwilling of the 'human group'. Consequently, those who fail to accept the American experience as being valid for all humanity are regarded, at best, as ignorant, at worst, as immoral. These attitudes lie at the root of intolerance at home and the demand for conformity to their economic and political ideas abroad. This intolerance, reinforced by her present economic and military power, breeds diabolical arrogance in America's relations with other nations. JP became aware of these inflexibly intolerant attitudes, clashed with them head on, and unwilling to be ideologically assimilated (as a black man he could not have expected to be socially assimilated), he was regarded as an ungrateful guest by his host. He was unceremoniously booted out of the United States.

E. U. Essien-Udom

Department of Political Science
University of Ibadan

INTRODUCTION

'You sure have a big chip on your shoulder!' I was often admonished by Americans, not least by the most unprivileged of them.

Being undilutedly black, and coming from a so-called undeveloped country and continent, I confess I must have felt and probably shall remain bitter at and jealous of all that passes and sells so loudly as western and white civilization, achieved as likely as not at the expense of the dark. And this was so with me going through Europe and England; America, my destination, just happened to be the limit, both of the dream and of the actuality of that achievement crying pride and power everywhere.

I should however like to state with all the emphasis and candour at my command that I went to the United States of America with a mind wide open and unpredisposed to prejudge, as well as with a sensibility neutral and on the ready to record and register all that came within reach of it. For me, hearing and hearsay were not going to be enough. I not only wanted to see things for myself while in America, I was determined right from when I jumped on the last plane in Lagos for New York that I would smell things out for myself, and made certain I would touch and taste to the full all that my bounteous host had to offer my kind. What follows therefore, the charitable might say, is not so much the story of my host and his incredibly sumptuous establishment but the jaundiced and unsavoury account of the responses and reactions of one difficult, hypercritical character and palate, who, presented with unusually rich grapes in a dish of silver and gold, took deprecatory bites, and churlishly spat everything out and in the face of all. Perhaps so. Now that I have got the whole fare out of my system, I feel so much better that I went through with the experience and the opportunity of that visit to America.

Undoubtedly, I proved myself a most awkward guest – so much so I have myself thought of simply calling this story 'The Awkward Guest' or 'Chips on my Shoulders'. I suppose this would have given my detractors and critics some measure of delight and satisfaction. But I have plumped for the present title for the simple reason that this is the kaleidoscope of America as I caught it in one academic year. The screen and view I hold up may appear warped and wanting correction, although I venture to insist the fault, if really it does not lie in the panorama itself, might very well be one shared by the operators who did the projecting of the pageant.

Otherwise Princeton and America were most generous and kind to me. Too much so, perhaps! Representative of both was the ex-Army Colonel and lecturer at Princeton, Dr Robert Van de Velde, together with his beautiful and spirited wife Barbara who advised and assisted him all the time. I had got myself invited to Princeton without knowing that it was through the sponsorship of two Nigerians then at Harvard and Princeton, namely Lawrence Ekpebu and my cousin Henry T. Bozimo. An American top advertisement man Richard Detwiler, a friend of mine, who some years before I had taken, as a civil servant, on an official tour of Western Nigeria, backed both boys up, and possibly more than any other person did a lot, by way of a regular correspondence with me in Nigeria, to persuade me to go to Princeton. And once there, the Colonel took me into his safe and firm keeping. A role like that instantly conjures up all that is crotchety, bilious, and grumpy. My Colonel, however, was quite the proverbial fairy father to me, a genie out of an Arabian tale. I had only to rub the lamp for him to emerge, large and unruffled, all set to perform the apparently impossible. Did I want to do a tour of the theatres from Broadway to the states and schools? Shake hands and dine with a live millionaire? Talk with a scientist who at Alamo had helped to build the split atom into what is today the greatest scare man has known since childhood? Or was it in the limelight of some film celebrity I would like to walk? Indeed, I only had to name my pet wish day by day, and the old war-horse was rearing to run me there. And didn't I, like the spoilt one I was, ride him hard!

True, I got thrown eventually, long before I saw all the wide, changing course of America, all expertly charted to by-pass the barricaded South, swing through the thirsty deserts and reserves of the Mid-West, past the fuming furnaces and forges up on the Great Lakes, and so West, down to the fabulous sunny terrains and gallops of California. But curse as much as I may still, I do not blame the Colonel for his impatience at last and my unexpected fall. Without riding the image to death, I guess I am what they call a heavy-footed fellow with an excitable turn of temper, and one therefore that would make at all times a poor jockey for the most trusty horse and sanguine backers and owner upon any field. I should be glad of another try!

Nor am I so naïve I want to suggest here a sharp undiscriminating picture of white against black, although Americans in spite of themselves do sometimes help to make it appear so. I did not come in contact exclusively with the politician, the salesman, or with the chauvinist-capitalist. The first would shake hands even with a week-old child, the second would sell the unemployed the latest washing-machine on the market, and the third turns every acre of his God-given land into a fighting frontier against all-comers. Of course, these characters are prominent on the turbulent American scene. It comes therefore as a relief to run into others on the field, who, no less native and loyal to the soil, do not clap you on the back, nor offer to sell you the underpants you already wear, nor challenge you to a fight on the spot for refusing to be converted to the cause of their particular clan and camp. I remember many such with respect. But I found the other side more important; so if the picture of America that you want to see is a rosy one, you had better stop reading this book now.

University of Ibadan   J. P. Clark
Ibadan
Nigeria

1 · INITIATIONS

At midnight one Wednesday night in May I fled the United States of America. Why that hour? Why the haste?

Having been shown the setting sun as I had been by my hosts at Princeton there was nothing more to do but take to the road, however dark, difficult and cold.

A very close circle of friends had stayed up that Wednesday night to see me off. Suddenly, Ruth Stone who was the life of it broke into a high, uneasy laugh: 'So the midnight flight is significant, after all! It's a reflection on your stay and experiences in the US!'

'Not a bad image!' I joined her. There we sat all six of us in the waiting room at Idlewild, now Kennedy Airport, Ruth and her husband Sam whose beautiful home at Great Neck on Long Island had its doors open to me come last or first train, Israel Rosenfield and Catherine Temeson, both of them young lovers and my constant companions in and out of college; and there was Chinua Achebe, my friend and fellow Nigerian writer, also then on some ticket to America, unlike mine just ended, a right and proper one from UNESCO.

None cared for any drink or talk although I ordered a beer

and insisted the others might at least each try a glass of cold water. So we just sat, some with knees touching and not quite looking each other in the eyes, until the insistent voice on the public address equipment said it was time passengers for London on the BOAC flight reported to their seats. That brought us all bolt-upright to our feet, and Ruth, who had got up this farewell group and given me some of my best days in the States, said simply: 'So you really are going, JP?' That must have been the tenth time of her asking inside ten minutes, but we all felt the urgency, and shook hands briefly, unable to talk. 'I'll be seeing you and Sam in July – in Nigeria,' I managed at last over my shoulders. 'And you, Israel, and Cat, make sure you enrol on the Peace Corps so you too can come over. Nigeria needs doctors and teachers.' And to Chinua I said: 'Countryman, come home soon; don't let them get you!'

They had all pressed after me past the Customs barriers, waving now and subdued somewhat, so that as the last doors shut between us, a certain screen seemed to spring into a place it had no right to be, and many times more oppressive than any wall in Berlin or ancient Benin. In that general nervousness I found, when I began belting myself in my seat, that I had left behind my overcoat. But, as the stewards said, there was little that could be done, except have it sent after me which they did, for already the huge vessel had begun moving, and before I knew there was any real racing going on, we were already off our feet, clear into the vast arms of blind space and night, forming yet another luminous body in the heavens. Below, the indeterminate sprawl of New York, a city with a dark heart, lay blinking and writhing with a thousand and one eyes like some mammoth centipede bruised upon the ground.

'What did I say,' giggled a middle-aged man at my elbow, 'no crashing with any plane I hop!'

'Shut up, honey!' his wife fixed him with a stare faster than all belts. There was scattered laughter down and up the corridor from among their friends and fellow passengers, all of them sporting placards labelled 'playboy' across their breasts, and no doubt going to do Europe, boys and bunnies all together. Turning away from the lot, I tried to engage myself with the new copy of *Ubu Roi* that Cat and Israel had given me as a parting gift only an hour or so back. But breathless as is that character's career, it could not win away my mind from the friends I had just left in the world's other half, faces which I felt I might well never see again.

Not quite a year before, I had alighted at the same airport on a broad milling afternoon. There was nobody at the ramp and waiting room to wave me in except the Immigration people. At first, they were surly and thorough, as expected, showing more than a fast hand and tongue as they ripped and riffled through my spare luggage.

'Any drugs?'

'No.'

'Any diamonds?'

'No.'

'What about gifts for friends?'

'None.'

'And money – how much have you got on you?'

Then one of them, with cap drawn over one eye, looked my passport over a second time, and without warning, hit me across the shoulder, quite viciously. Now, what terrible discovery has he made? I wondered. But I shouldn't have worried, for the fellow hit me another one and asked aloud with a big laugh: 'So you got a Fellowship to Princeton!'

'Boy, oh boy!' chimed in his colleague, 'You know that's one of our top colleges!'

And instantly they all made me plenty welcome.

'Call any cab out there and it will take you safe into the city,' one offered.

'But be sure you fix the fare first before going,' his mate took over. 'And go straight to Penn Station if you are going direct to Princeton. It's right on the other side – in New

Jersey State.' All of which advice they offered completely free
of charge, and when I said 'Thank you' they all answered in
one voice: 'Oh, you're welcome!'

Incidentally, I had no need of a taxi cab, jumping a lift off
some Nigerian diplomat at the United Nations. There were
three of us in the car besides him, all of us Nigerians. First
was the friend he had come to collect, a young lawyer, fresh
from London and going to Yale for another year's study. The
other, it turned out, was a civil servant from Lagos enrolled
on the same programme that was taking me to Princeton.
Three of us newcomers felt rather lost in the capacious holds
of the car. 'You dare not, as a public servant, take this home
with you unless of course you want to set up yourself against
the politicians in power and their retainers,' I teased the
diplomat. 'Just look out there,' was all he said as we swept
into the multiple cross current of cars. His, I came to concede,
was anything but spacious and serpentine compared with the
average vehicle on the road, but then at home it would be
ostentatious living all the same, as only politicians and their
conmen can afford. 'You see, you are in the United States,'
he said. It was a reminder I was to hear rubbed into me again
and again like salt over a sore for several months to come.

New York City was too much with me driving into it that
open and warm afternoon. Of course, I had expected to see
steel and glass structures, all shining bright, rise slender and
beautiful before my eyes. But what struck me immediately
was the dust and smut covering the face of New York, and
one not exactly that of the ages as has settled for good upon a
place like London or Paris. At first, it was hard for me to
place or breathe, perhaps because strange, primitive pictures
were at that time stirring in my mind. For example, I had
for quite some time the uncanny vague feeling of being
borne in a boat into the heart of some heavily wooded group
of islands, each singing out its special charms – and yet one
looked so much like the other – and in my mind's ears all the
time was some united and commingled sound of the long and

dull splash of fish barely surfacing and of the brush and crack
of twigs and bush giving way before some shadowy animals
criss-crossing before my eyes. And superimposed over all
this, more pressing and overpowering, was the picture of
Columbus and his unknown band of desperate sailors, several
hundreds of years before, bearing down in their big billowing
boats upon surprised bands of Red Indians who took those
strange vessels for huge birds sent by their great lord from
heaven. How had the man done it? I kept asking myself.
Today, in a monster more like those huge birds of heaven the
foredoomed Red Indians wondered at, it takes the better part
of the day to make the Atlantic crossing to America, which
for better or for worse, all the world now knows is irrevocably
there. 'How had the man done it? I kept asking myself more
in sincere rhetoric than actual hope of a practical answer.

However, a friend at Northwestern University up in the
State of Illinois soon brought me back to earth. Coming into the
great harbour of New York with the famous Statue of Liberty
holding out to all the weary and oppressed of the earth her
hand flaming gold, he wrote to me, how could anybody but
the daft Columbus miss the way to the heart of America? As
I had already had the terrible misfortune of missing the way,
so to speak, I thought it best not to argue the point, especially
that portion of it implying all and everyone coming to the
States today must be either hungry, weary or oppressed.

Undoubtedly, my first impressions of America as seen
through the city of New York were overlush and typical of
the jungles from which I understood I had just emerged. Soon
after, they were to dissolve into terms and images more
easily recognizable to the civilized. They even resolved into
verse. The first of these pieces sees New York as a warehouse
cum machine factory –

> Steel, stone, glass boxes! Not one
> A carton
> To handle with care!

Castellated, crowd
Miles on end, fall one
Over the other, and Empire State, the proud
Peak flying a pennon
Above this nightmare
Of ladders, beams, bolts, fumes, refuse . . .
And below!
America, Broadway, Madison,
Park, Lexington
And all the other streets
And avenues, east and west,
In a blue splash of steel
Cascade over channels, drop tubes past
Collisions of shafts, are
Sparking conveyor belts, turning,
Churning, carrying like rapids
The boil and market of a continent
Incontinent . . .
So rears
The anthill
Into the rainbow sky –
The intercellar city, the tail
In the mouth files of anonymous
Citizens overburdened with work,
The soldiers guarding well
Beyond the gates, each
Together, severally
And equally
For the commonweal

But here,
Where is the care,
   the pool,
      the queen?

Another, at once more obvious and oblique pictures the

city as some promiscuous, chic client of neon-lit night clubs –

> A dumpling by day
> At night a fairy
> In a dance of stars

And yet a third, almost an epigraph, writes off the great iron heap in rather funeral terms –

> The skyscrapers and
> Bridges, among the avenues
> And isles, are pyramids
> And aqueducts, cutting
> Swathes on a tired ground
> Saddling streams running to sand.

Admittedly, these are all uncharitable remarks, but driving through the many-storeyed mounds and obelisks of New York, all of them set out in their square lots and rows, and then running every now and again past its vast, sprawling burial grounds with all those spendid tombs and tablets, several of them decked with fresh flowers and flying flags, authentic versions of the star-spangled banner, the eye tired of looking upon stone and glass forms, whether squat or slender, and the fact became more blurred in the mind as to which structure and block was put up to the dead and which to the living.

At long last night came. Leaving London earlier in the day, the gimmick had been that you take off at 11.30 a.m. and touch down five hours later at exactly the same hour in New York. Actually we did not arrive till almost double that time. By then we had been served lunch in the air. But what with the weird protraction of day going west I was to have yet another lunch, a regular Nigerian dish of jolof rice and stewed chicken, washed down by long draughts of cold beer. The effect was to the restore the bottom which I sort of felt and feared had dropped out of my being. One of those interminable parties at the United Nations was going on that night, and my old school friend, into whose apartment I had moved, after his initial grumble at not being warned in good time of my coming, brightened up on the second Bourbon and ginger, and it was in that expansive spirit, he suggested I come along with him. I demurred, said I needed a good warm bath, and that even a vigil long as that for an elder of the clan gone home had to come to an end sometime.

As it happened, I kept further vigil on that my first night in the United States. I was curled up in the bath, splashing and singing to myself, (spluttering it was more like), when the telephone rang in the sitting room. 'Let it,' I muttered above the suds. 'Whoever is calling will hang up soon enough.' But the buzz-buzzing noise of it went on, and worse than that of a fly or mosquito, it was futile trying to beat it off my ears. So cursing and sopping wet, I put about me the towel nearest to hand and padded out into the bedroom to take the call there. The voice at the other end was that of a woman obviously heavy with caresses – more for her own self.

'No, he isn't in,' I told her. 'You saw him at the party, did you say? . . . I see . . . He stopped at yours . . . Yes, I am the guest just from Africa . . . You told him you'd come and keep me company? Wasn't that real sweet of you! Oh, no, I can't believe you are a tough nut at all . . . Really? You mean right now? How wonderful! Hold on, I don't know the number off-hand . . . That's good, I forgot you know the place yourself . . . Well, bye-bye then till ten.'

For what appeared the arrested hand of time I held up the receiver in the air gulping and ogling at it – just as soulfully as they do in the films. Here was a sudden burst of a torch out from the dark, and though blinking somewhat, I told myself I would follow it wherever it led, even at the risk of stumbling upon mound or pit. The sideboard of an expatriate, whether colonial or consular, is his sure comforter. So diving into my host's which even by diplomatic standards was pretty well stocked, I poured myself a drink and settled down to watch television until the arrival of my surprise visitor.

A closer look, however, at the Maverick strip that was running then, one that showed the rascal bursting the ring of some ruthless bank-busters led by his old flame, who entertains the Wild West crowd in the pub below to belly dancing while the deed is being done upstairs, and I was sure I had seen the episode before on TV – months and months ago back home in Nigeria. I picked up the weekly programme to find something fresh to turn to. It told a similar story. *Dr Kildare, Cheyenne, Laramie, Bonanza, The Loretta Young Show, People are Funny*, and all the other drug-peddling, punch-packing, cow-poaching, bust-flaunting and dollar-spilling serials, exported as ceaselessly to stations in Nigeria as they are sedulously decried by Yankees there as anything but poor specimens of the real products at home, all of them filled the bills and were actually in many cases touted as the highlights of viewing for the teenager, the adult, and indeed the entire family. All of them which made me feel rather at home.

So that I felt more or less rattled when my mysterious caller turned up and said she was Australian. She asked me to help her out of her overcoat, a sort of ritual over here, I was to discover, expected of anyone playing host. A touch of winter was in the weather, she said, so she had had to wear a medium-weight one. By the time I had found where to hang it up, she had sat herself down on the couch, and turned off the TV set, saying, 'Could we put on some records instead?'

I said, 'Oh yes, and what will Madam drink?'

'Scotch and no soda,' she said, 'and please no Madams either, the name is Grace, and what is yours?'

She turned out more curious than gracious, asking one question after another when I had not answered the first, at least, to my satisfaction. 'So you are a journalist and dabble in

poetry and plays?' She gave me a squint-type of look. She
knew a couple of poets down in Greenwich Village, and was
it poetry I was going to teach at Princeton? I repeated again
that the fellowship taking me there was not a teaching one,
nor a studying one exactly, 'but one, and I quote,' I added,
'aimed at bringing talented young men from the new and
developing nations of the world so that they can improve on
their capabilities and be better able to serve their countries –'

'And the USA, of course!' she laughed, teasing the words
off my lips.

'Aren't you a real witch?' I swept up to her, using the
chance to plant myself more advantageously by her side.

'Oh, nothing of the sort,' she shook her well coiffeured
hair, all brilliant and bronze, and which she was prompt to
point out was all hers. 'I have worked for one or two foreign
missions here and come across that type of crap talk. Pretty
catching stuff.'

'You work for some mission here?' I began.

'Oh, nothing much, honey!'

She cupped my chin in her free hand, and holding out the
other, asked if I wasn't going to recharge her glass any more.

'Of course, yes.'

I bounded up to where the bottles stood, each by now
showing a decided drop in the level. In the meantime,
however, her interest had shifted to the layout of the apartment, one of those extra-convenient and well-cushioned caves
quarried out of square blocks of mountains of steel, stone and
glass they call apartment blocks. She was thinking of
moving out of hers into something still more padded from
care. I offered to show her around, and although half-
protesting she already could tell her way about the place,
she allowed herself to be led, and so it was we found ourselves
in one of the bedrooms.

'I wondered when you were coming to that,' was all she
said when I fell upon her. 'Sex to the American,' she said,
taking off her jacket, blouse, skirt, chemise, corset, stockings

and bra with a method and care that showed a mind most clear even at the moment of crisis, was the twin sister of the Almighty Dollar; and high and low, young and old, men and women over here were all slaves to it. 'Why, only the other day,' she went on 'some big shot drove up in his Cadillac. He had his two kid sons with him, one a little over twenty and the younger just turned eighteen or thereabouts. 'You make love to the boys,' he offered, 'and here's two hundred bucks for your trouble.'

'Two hundred for initiating two dumb kids?' I started.

'Oh, that's nothing to them,' she soothed my spine. 'Sex is their highest commodity, and they have made the thing so synthetic and commercial, love has become a changeable ware. And the more perverted it is, the more expensive.'

'Still,' I began, but she cut into my stream of thoughts which at that moment was running down all sorts of grooves in an effort to determine if all this wasn't merely a lead I was expected to follow.

'Wait,' she said, 'you haven't heard the really funny part of the story yet.'

'And what's that?' I asked.

'Oh, as he collected his kids to go back to his ranch, or some place, he stopped and whispered into my ear something to the effect that tomorrow would be Daddy's own day.'

'A very practical man,' I said and switched off the bed-lamp.

'Yes, they all are,' she agreed.

Of the antiques and antics that account for a great deal of Princeton I had had tips and hints well before arriving at the place. In fact, one day after my checking into campus, an American with whom I had made friends some time back in Nigeria asked me over to his home out in a wooded, prosperous suburb of New York.

It happened to be Culture Day. The Lincoln Centre, a multibillion dollar affair, was having its official opening with a big gala performance by Leonard Bernstein and his boys. Naturally, some of the heat generated there flowed into every true American family and home, as indeed was the case at the house of my friend Richard Detwiler, a vice-president at the Madison Avenue giant advertising firm of Batten, Barton, Durstine and Osborn Inc., who create public images for clients as different and as distinguished as former US Vice-President Richard Nixon and the Western Nigeria Government of Chief S. L. Akintola. So all that day at my host's we heard Robert Frost read his poems, one of which, about a wall, written many years before, the shrewd old man had only just found fame for at an impromptu reading to Kruschev in Moscow; and we drank coffee with real English muffins, in the glow of a bright wooden fire struck up by the young heir-apparent of the house; and when some neighbour dropped in, we listened to him talk of the Newport boat race which had just ended with the Americans coming as it were from behind to beat their gallant Australian challengers. Apparently, the highlight of it all for the man, who was something of an expert in this time-honoured maritime event, was seeing President Kennedy watch the historic race in his own yacht.

The TV set in the living room wouldn't work and equally temperamental was that upstairs. Anyway, for a few awkward sequences during which the sales stunts Dick's firm did for a glass firm featured prominently, as part of their bargain for sponsoring the great civic ceremony, we were able to see the Lincoln Festival at that point when Governor Rockefeller or his brother, one or the other of whom was officiating, got lost somehow in the huge gleaming edifice, and the microphones and cameras, like prehensile equipment trained by men from Mars were kept purring and whirring in vain search of their target. And for supper, there was raw steak, rather redolent of human flesh, I told them, real fresh vegetable juice, with all the vitamins intact, iced in tall glasses reached by straws, and dessert of apple pie baked by the young daughter of the house, ten years old if a day. After which I was packed off to bed upstairs in my host's spare pair of pyjamas in which I floundered all night. And the morning after, before we drove up to connect with the underground into the city, everybody said: 'Oh, come again!'

All of which formed a fine prelude to Princeton. Yet I still was not quite prepared for the original thing. If New York is some overgrown, gross, ugly hostess, stalking on stilts, retiring to bed with her wig on, and with more than her bosom lifted and powdered freely, if she throws garden parties in and out of season while thousands hunger at the gates, Princeton is a regular bachelor, fortyish and therefore most foolish in his pretences and professions. He has more than two hundred million dollars stowed away safe in gilt-edge holdings on Wall Street and two or so panjandrums watch over the progress on the stock market. More, the stumping of over-opulent, cigar-chumping and very high blood-pressured uncles is ever present in his ears. About the time of my admission within his gates, some $64 million had just come into his purse and pocket by his mere appeal to relations that part of the family house needed extension. On top of this, one cranky uncle, directing his name be not made public, perhaps for fear of outsiders pestering him thereafter, gave all by himself a gift of $35 million for the rebuilding of the Woodrow Wilson sector of the estate. How many sovereign states today want but a fraction of that to feed their impoverished millions! And wide-girdled frothy-fronted aunts, several of them dowagers, when not visiting some hospital or home, inmates of which their own greed and graft had served to wreck, keep a vigilant watch on the ward so that no mean adventurer slips into the garden to sow seeds of corruption. And, gracious beings that they are, the old ladies are always sponsoring some bazaar in aid of the poor, always playing hostess at some tea party or another.

It was my great misdemeanour to miss one such high party, worse still, right at the beginning of my Princeton career. This was a welcome party given by some Hospitality Committee for the benefit of students and fellows from foreign lands and on behalf of Princeton University and community. And I failed to show up for it!

'Where were you? Mr and Mrs So-and-So called to take you in their automobile to the party. You were looked for everywhere. Actually cabled to Lagos but lost track of you in Freetown or some such place. Every other person was there,' Dr Robert Van de Velde who was to run my life for the rest of my stay in the States fired away at me. An old army colonel, with none of his colours faded, he gave me no quarter and actually manoeuvred my rout at the end.

I said I was sorry, that I didn't myself know I would accept the invitation to come to Princeton until the very day I left home, that I had stopped over at Accra, Monrovia, Freetown, Las Palmas, but that none of them had caused my delay. The real cause was that some well-meaning American friends had stopped me in the city to perform initiation rites into the great American way of life. 'Well,' he growled, 'you go and report to the Graduate School and have yourself properly registered. Your friends have all done so.'

My friends on the course, when I came to sift the list out of a fat sheaf of hand-outs left at the porters' lodge for me, made quite a fine bunch. Besides my fellow Nigerian, there was a diplomat and cabinet secretary from Syria, an assistant editor of Warsaw's political magazine, another journalist from South Korea, a young demi-semi diplomat from Yugoslavia, connected with some government research work in his country and whose father was Tito's envoy to Indonesia, an army general in charge of police duties and security in the Republic of Somalia, a young graduate of Dakar University teetering between an academic life and a diplomatic career in the service of Dahomey, and a deputy director of agricultural extension services for Haiti who at the time of our parting was considering relinquishing his post at home in Duvalier's domain for one in the Congo, Leopoldville. This was the talented group into which Princeton set out to instil the spirit and miracle of the American achievement while sharpening the individual skill of each for him to do a better job of work back home.

How did the old crotchety bachelor come by this brilliant idea? Such a healthy, outward-looking and productive seed does not derive from the masturbating dreams that an inward-turned, nail-pairing celibate enters into in the sufficiency of his self-milking estate. It is now the traditional story over there where customs form fast and as finely as cobwebs, and one often told with watery eyes and with a good smack of lips by those tending the remarkable culture, that the whole affair started when Mr Justice Douglas, an Associate Judge of the Supreme Court of the United States, was invited to deliver some annual course of lectures at Princeton.

The theme he chose was America challenged, and it had thrown into sharp, fresh focus old queries such as: why had Americans slept while Senator McCarthy was spotting witches in every nook and corner of their homes? Why should American youth with all its heritage of George Washington who never lied and Thomas Jefferson who more than any single founder penned the famous declaration of independence be asked to take the oath of allegiance before being granted state bursaries? And can America sincerely and successfully continue projecting abroad, especially to the new nations of Africa and Asia, her image of a great democracy that guarantees to each citizen freedom, justice, wealth and more, when it appears cracking up right here at home?

It needed a brave, free mind to raise these questions right there in the tiger's lair, for Princeton is the proud custodian of all that is America, beautiful and perfect. And there perhaps the matter might have died had not Princeton, in one of those rare quirks of mind that turn otherwise sedate, delicate dilettanti into intemperate and possessed champions of lost causes, decided to publish the lectures together in book form. The beautifully brought out volume got into the hands of a grand old man up on the West Coast who wrote to the distinguished author down in Washington, who apprised Princeton of the simple pointed questions asked by the man with the money: how can one American help to improve matters between the US and the world?

'Several ways.' The honourable judge tossed his grey mane.

'Name one, and I have the money to pay for it,' said the millionaire up in California. And so it was the Parvin Programme began, that these past two years has attracted to Princeton and the United States of America a steady stream of talented young men from all over the world.

The Graduate College of Princeton University, where members of the group were billeted, provides a fine specimen of the anachronistic set-up that is Princeton. The name, like many things here, is rather misleading as the place is nothing more than a hall of residence, although, as they are quick and proud to point out, the first residential graduate college in all America. Centred around a quadrangle cut off into an inner and front court, the Graduate College dates from President Woodrow Wilson. In fact, it was the building of it in 1913 where it stands today that drove the scholar Wilson to seek fresh new pastures, a step that took him first to the governorship of New Jersey and then to the presidency of the United States of America, from which aerial pedestal the man saw visions of a world that must unite at once to his call and under his lead or remain for ever beleaguered by division and distrust.

The heavy bust of Dean West, who won the day against the twice disillusioned President, all because he knew the way to the heart and purse of Princeton's benefactors, sits solid and square today in the forecourt, dominating the lawn as if in perpetual grouse against all latter day masters of the hall. Over it hangs an air of solitary splendour, perhaps symbolic of the fact that the Graduate College, which he sired out in the woods and outskirts of the great estate, right out on the

terrain where the Battle of Princeton was fought in 1777, remains today somewhat removed from the centre of things in the family – which is rather a pity, as a brush or two with his weather-beaten tenants, drawn from other climes, should prove a fine tonic for the young gentlemen who in the main campus delight a great deal in punch and punch-bowl.

Dinner for inmates at the Graduate College, all of whom live in entries, is quite an occasion. Gowns must be worn and these over anything from football jerseys to army and navy jungle shorts and boots. A French professor of mathematics, once doing a term at Princeton, is said to have carried the practice one night to its strict logical conclusion by appearing at dinner absolutely nude under his brief gown. Apparently, nobody was amused; the grand ritual has simply gathered more cobwebs since. Academic gowns are however a slight veneer. In this stronghold of Presbyterians and Unitarians graces are still proudly said in Latin, (which sounded like pidgin Latin to me). And Procter Hall for which all this homage has been ordained lacks but one thing: a moat on the outside. Its high-arched and vaulted ceilings, its stained windows, its great chandeliers, (which Dickens probably would have likened to tears of some ogrish woman had he stopped there on either of his two trips to God's own country), its heavy oak-panelled walls with pictures, framed larger than life, of some dead that were no Bacon, Milton or Newton, all these and more are attributes and apparels that may sit well upon living matriarchs like Cambridge and Oxford. But upon a misogynist like Princeton gone completely bald although still hairless between the thighs, the effect appears terribly grotesque.

And to complete this noonday masquerade, there is the big gothic Grover Cleveland Memorial Tower, the tallest point in all Princeton. Its chiming bells sometimes require the services of experts, the last of whom was hired all the way from a dying guild in the Netherlands. Every Sunday and holiday, tourist crowds, from outside Princeton and beyond the State of New Jersey, flock to gaze at this famous structure, and the thrill sent through them is great indeed, even like the clear silver waves of the musical bells themselves, when those relics of a renaissant Europe, all hidden away in the heavenly heights of the tower, break over them into some quaint hymn, however out of key.

Princeton with its towers, cupolas, turrets, frescoes and columns is one grand museum of architectural titbits down the ages. A stop in front of any, and its ivy-covered façade clamours forth an epoch, and the brash visitor has but to knock on the heavy grimy double doors, and echoes of some epic known only to Princeton resound down the tall vaults and spacious corridors.

Nassau Hall deservedly provides the centre to the close circle of the college. Built in 1756, it easily is the oldest of the institutions, carries most history, and even in those early remote days offered the largest single academic structure in all the colonies. Bearing the royal name of William III, the building changed hands in quick turns between loyalist and rebel troops until its final fall to George Washington. And it was within its walls, still standing today after two fires and so many sieges, that the General received the thanks of that Congress which actually occupied the hall as the capitol of the country for six months. Although now mainly used for faculty meetings and special ceremonies, this famous hall, at one time containing all of Princeton, has not entirely shed its military character. Names of all Princetonians who have fallen in service of their country are inscribed there. Outside on the front steps bronze tigers crouch and growl at all intruders in true Princetonian fashion, and commanding the central quadrangle is a cannon, a relic of the Revolutionary War, and it is around it that seniors hold their last class exercises.

In contrast to this leathery and scarred colonial monster, both Clio and Whig halls, one formerly and the other currently the headquarters of the oldest student literary and debating club in America, may well be mistaken for ancient Greek and Roman temples with transplanted columns, façade and frescoes from across the Atlantic. And the twins do not go beyond the turn of the century.

Even younger still is the Harvey S. Firestone Memorial Library, a rambling, castellated castle with enough shelters to save the high-destined gentlemen of Princeton from the nuclear sacrifice they know will consume others. For me, however, Firestone gave no security. On my way to America, I had stopped in Liberia and seen the one huge rubber plantation Harvey Firestone has made of it. All that land had at one time been made over to the Pan-Africanist prophet Marcus Garvey. But the combined powers of the United States, Great Britain and France disapproved of his plan of settling the coloured people of America in the midst of subject Africans. So instead, Firestone inherited the vast lots, and Garvey headed for jail and oblivion. And for his co-operation, the great, interested powers were gracious enough to invest the President of Liberia with several honours and gifts.

Today it is Princetonians, and not young Liberians in any appreciable size, who enjoy part of the abundant harvest of Harvey S. Firestone. Yes, every book I plucked out of shelves in there brought the taste of ash to my tongue. But then for the owners, these are what they call endowments, benefits and donations. Indeed the gracious living of the rich and the civilized gives rise to the disgraceful conditions in the lower depths of the earth. But they also furnish those charms that have helped to earn for Princeton an honourable position in that holy American trinity whose other members are Harvard and Yale.

Considering all that ivy crawling over its face, Princeton is a place hardly in need of bouquets from an outsider and rustic. All the same I offered a couple, but these were thought brickbats by those who regard the place a shrine. *Autumn in Princeton*, the first of them, goes like this:

The leaves, so golden, shower
In the wind. And each tree,
Antlered, stands
A silhouette to prick the eye:
Chilling as are hands
That lash up the drift, oh may I
Never be caught unaware,
Or cast off root, bole and bower,
When the touch falls on me.

Two others, written when winter had invested all with
chill and the grip of ice, speak of –

The elm trees, still
Shaven bald and gaunt,
In the brief buba
They wear after the snow,
Are a band of alufa
Deployed down the neighbourhood – and ask of –
Snow,
      Away
From my window
By the time of waking,
      What deft, gentle hands spread
      You over this bed
Of bile, while we slept? And say,
Nurse, when shall the corpse lie?
    There, ding, dong, ding –
When all the world is a mushroom pie.

Spring, when it came, after all the clean shaving and
sheathing that were autumn and winter, gave the impression
of a bald person suddenly growing back his hair. And although
the almost overnight burst of green springing out like one
huge parasol all over the place made every true native heart
exult, mine that was of the rain forests of Nigeria, where all

the year round they never lose their colour, remained somewhat dampened of spirit. Rather, strange as it may sound, I missed the old dry colonial canals cutting through Princeton, especially at that season when dry leaves covered them up in rustling arms, and I also missed the bare, brown fields outside the gates which all through autumn into winter carried the look of dry, clotted blood, just as they must have looked when the Great George Washington stole up one gibberish Christmas night, and chopped up in their sleep on this very terrain the German sots and swine that were the royal army of George III. I even walked among the big, broken pillars left lying close by the grounds of the Graduate College. The old mansion, to which they had once offered support as well as pride, had already long been pulled down. But someone, too late, had then thought better of it and given orders that the columns should not be carted away but left lying there in sweet remembrance of things past. An ancient battlefield, and several huge fallen pillars: between them, they provide a fine heraldry and crest for Princeton.

2 · DAYS WITH THE DAILIES

What becomes of the copy
Unused? The sheaves gathered more
In jest than sweat, and
Winnowed to the grain? Those facts
And figures, so carefully
Abstracted, dressed to a table
For consumption at breakfast
Or tea-time? The story
Turned into a tale,
Plain, tall or crooked, depending
To what end or floor
It was tracked – Does the copy
Not led
To bed,
However harriedly, just as children
Or patients when they brood strike,
Does it, upon its spike,
Hope, like some holy man
Of the East, to enter
Into the ALL, or
Does the poor copy,

Undelivered, more
Like the stillborn lying
In the morgue for study,
Forever drift a ghost?

These were lines I wrote to tease a friend working for some big news agency in Washington. Because he was covering President Kennedy's State of the Union message to Congress, he had been unable to extend me the hospitality of his home during my first visit to the capital. The pity of it, he later wrote to apologise, was that the story he had done at such great strain and sacrifice was not used by a single newspaper he knew of. It appeared none liked the tone of it – which inclined to the flippant. But could it be that the story was not even fed out in the first instance? News management was the order of the day then in Washington, and in this matter of standing up for the flag and the constitution, the division is pretty thin between the government and the press, which, as well as being big business in its own right, provides a proper trumpet for the grand triumphant march that is America.

I never quite got to know for although I paid several more visits to Washington I did not have that reunion with my friend which both of us had so much set our hearts on. Something seemed to come between us which made for a steady drifting apart. I dwell on this because it turned out to be symptomatic of my relationship with the various newspapers and editors I met with in America. First, there was great warmth and a feeling of fellowship; then an inexplicable freeze, followed by a feeling of disaffection on both sides, even of frustration and anger.

The first of these meetings, right at the college level, took place at Princeton and more or less by accident. I had dropped in at the University Store to pick up a fresh stock of handkerchiefs, pants, tooth-paste and soap, all of them articles which I seemed to shed behind me wherever I stopped for the night, when my cousin and guide, first of the new crop of African and black students now altering the lily-white face of Princeton, grabbed me and said: 'How would you like to see the student newspaper?'

'Fine,' I said. 'And how far from here?'

'It's right inside this building,' he laughed, 'right at the back in fact.'

So we took the steps up, and before we were on the landing bumped into a red-faced youth. 'Oh, want to see *The Princetonian*?' he offered. We said yes. 'I am just a reporter here, you know,' he laughed again. 'But come on in and see our chairman.'

We followed hot on his heels, into a room all rolls and stacks, and there pondering over some opinion on the editorial desk, was a big beardless fellow who between the tap-tap of his pencil against his teeth, said he wasn't exactly the boss of the place, but that he was a top brass there was no denying. Whether publisher, editor-in-chief, president or some other such post, as all papers here seem to have, I can't quite recall now. But I remember his fixing me to the door with the steady projectile of his pale bluish eyes when my cousin said something to the effect that I work on a newspaper back home in Nigeria.

'What paper?' the young newspaper executive asked, tap-tapping at his teeth.

I gave the name and was not surprised it made no impression on him.

'What is your circulation?' he asked, and because the pencil had stopped somewhat against the enamel of his teeth, there was a sound like the hiss of a snake to his innocent question.

'About 75,000,' I remember saying.

'That's very respectable,' the up-and-coming brass said approvingly. And that ended the interview, for as he put it, they were very busy that afternoon.

The Princetonian is a real chip off the old block. If its fine type and texture of the paper are calculated to recall *The New*

York Times and perhaps *The Christian Science Monitor* in Boston, the photo size and bold exposure it holds up to the reader certainly go back to the tabloid tradition. A fine mixture of airs pardonable in student journalism, except that everybody here takes everything so seriously, and will not be second to anybody in the honourable role of upholding America the bounteous and beautiful. In the last presidential elections, the paper, a true voice of the thoroughbreds that fill the Princeton stable, opted for the Republican jockey, Richard Nixon. And as evidence of the healthy cross-current of that old democratic spirit flowing through the woods and halls of Princeton, it is only fair to report that a majority of the staff stood up manfully for the Democrat runner, John Kennedy. Not that it makes a difference either way.

But the phenomenon of healthy disagreement reflecting the widest will of the people showed in its most robust form over the Cuban crisis. Apparently, a division of opinion had developed among members of the editorial committee. To accommodate this, there had to be a follow-up of opinion expressed the day before, a complete right-about-turn by this time, and all duly signed by its authors or signatories in the grand tradition of the Bill of Rights that, like Marvells' inevitable chariot of time, is for ever charging at the back of every true American mind. This was a fresh and brilliant performance indeed to come from adolescents, considering that the elders and adults through the entire course and field gave of nothing spectacular but hot puffs of breath and the heavy tread of unanimous feet. Still, *The Princetonian* can huff too, when it comes to it, and this pretty often enough and on all sorts of occasions. 'You should all go and see *Galileo* with your dates,' it once pronounced judgment in a preview carried under the editorial column, 'although the author of the play, the German Bertolt Brecht, is a damned Communist.'

And yet on another occasion, in a great burst of service to the community, which like many another in the United States will do anything today to contain the skeleton of

racial relations now tumbling out of its long-shut-up cup-
board, *The Princetonian* had a zestful social scientist do a
survey of what the students at the university think of Jews
and Negroes in this day and age. The last time there was a
tally like that on the campus was more than a generation
back, when Paul Robeson was refused admission by the
college on account of his colour. Different standards were
adopted for each of the sets of questionnaires distributed, and
all of them tacitly understood against a backdrop of those
absolutes that go to make a true Yankee. Thus for the Jews,
there were leading questions like: do you think they are
industrious? Are they intelligent? Do they insist on their
pound of flesh? And for the Negro, typical of the questions
were: are they musical? Do they show a tendency to idle?
Aren't those people sloppy and slovenly?

Needless to say, in this stupid game of mixed-up rules and
rigged results, the odds showed the Jews in the eyes of the
élite at Princeton had made strides deserving of a review of
that quota system still used to keep them and the blacks out
of Princeton. The shadow of Albert Einstein at the nearby
Institute of Advanced Study probably had something to do
with it! All African students, in the absence of Negro under-
graduates at Princeton, felt furious that the best of American
young minds should still regard the black members of their
society as slovenly, idle, and musical in the pejorative sense
of that word. But they apparently thought better of it and
kept the lid firm on the boiling pot of their discontent. A wag
among them well summed up the whole incident when he
said: 'Their grandfathers ate yam like everyone else, but
thought it cooked by the gods themselves, and today so do
their heirs. For how else can the tribe continue?'

From this collegiate start I graduated to the county level.
This time there was some preparation on both sides of the
fence. In the interval, however, at a tea-party given by the
English-Speaking Union, Princeton Chapter, at Dean
Hamilton's residence, Wyman House, for incoming students

was that we had agreed that the promotions manager back in the press in New Brunswick would call me later that week to arrange where and at what hour and on what bus he should meet me. It was this call I had missed because I had in the meantime sandwiched a visit to New York. I missed the right train returning, but got on the telephone at once to my Princeton sponsor and the publisher, and at that time, everybody said: 'Oh, it doesn't matter at all!'

Publisher Boyd, fiftyish, crinkly about the eyes, and very sprightly, well confirmed that old saying that small bottles usually carry good wine. This was not the first time he had played host to an African journalist. As a matter of fact, a Nigerian editor had spent some time on his paper a year or so back and was wanting at that time to return to the States. Did I know him? I said I did, and when I added the paper I worked for before coming was part-owned by Nigerians and part-owned by the Canadian press mogul Roy Thomson, his Irish eyes lit up. And did I know the old rogue was even then in New York? No, I said. Has he come to carry off some more newspaper chains, the old rogue with itchy fingers? Which made even our old colonel join in our laughter. A conscientious democrat, (as a matter of fact he was chairman of his local party branch), the colonel manoeuvred the topic to the influence a paper like that of our friend was likely to exert on the course of voting in Congress and the local elections which were then in the offing down the entire sweep of the land.

'We are not partisan,' the press baron said, 'but we do make it a point of the duty we owe the country and community we serve to examine candidates on their individual merits. It is on the basis of this we recommend to the electorate the acceptance or rejection of any candidate put up by either of the parties.'

'A very good policy,' the colonel nodded his hectagonal head in approval.

And before the small conference broke up, there was some

talk that it would be a good thing if my proposed tour of the press could take in some newspaper chains out in the Mid-West. These had a character and a colour all their own, and the publisher who had the necessary connections said he would only be too pleased to put me in touch. I lost that opportunity.

The Home News, true to its name, has all the family and close community atmosphere of a house magazine, but a very prosperous one indeed. Serving the twin counties of Middlesex and Somerset with a population of about half a million between them, its readership of more than 40,000, come weekday or Sunday, forms part of the garden state of New Jersey now fast turning itself into one vast suburban sprawl between the two metropolitan centres of New York and Philadelphia, America's two giant, ancient cities on the east coast. The paper is understandably very proud of the fact that the average family income of $7,000 enjoyed by its readers stands out as one of the highest buying powers in the whole of the United States. Thus it carries every day a heavy tonnage of advertisements, covering in the course of the year more than a million inches of linage worth its weight in gold.

I became fast friends with the paper's promotion manager John Donnelly. He showed me the whole house from the editorial section to the press room, where a brand new Scot Press sported six units. There they stood sleek, sturdy and restive like stallions all set for a race. The editorial page editor, Mr Alexander Jones, also gave me generously of his time and knowledge. Ours was a meeting on common ground, to quote the beautiful story the paper did on my visit. And between him and the management there was a happy meeting of minds. As a result, there hardly was any split in opinion he could think of, and in any case, a good number of the editorials, like feature and news stories, were syndicated stuff that came in by teleprinter or post. In the women's department, two perfectly charming girls explained to me the smooth working of their page. A lot of this was taken up by wedding photographs and stories. Both girls were somewhat startled when I likened their job to that of compiling albums of social events. Oh, not really, they demurred, and how was the job done on my own paper? They would love to see a Nigerian newspaper, you know, they said. I promised I would let them, not that there was anything much to show, but all the same, I said I would. Much to my shame, the promise was never fulfilled.

All told, the mail room left on me the most happy impression. As the finished paper is spat out in elevens every one second, it is taken on conveyor belts from the press to the mail room for bundling in proper numbers, then for tying, and finally the bundles are carried on endless belts to trucks waiting outside to make delivery to newsstands and the five hundred newsboys serving the two counties. The entire operation is automatic, swift, smooth and seemingly endless to watch. Here, I told my hosts, was something we could certainly do with in my native land.

Pleasant as my stay at *The Home News* was, one or two minor incidents occurred that more or less clogged for me its oiled flow. The first, very slight and unnoticed by anyone, was my meeting in the cafeteria with a well-groomed capsule-sized youth.

'Come and meet our guest from Nigeria,' the gentleman who was standing me lunch called out to him. 'This is Boyd Junior, our President's son,' he told me. We shook hands, a bit limply perhaps, and Boyd Junior walked away immediately to collect his meal.

'I thought he was one of your cub reporters,' I said, looking at the young man now part of the general body of workers jostling for their lunch.

'Well, so he is,' my friend said simply, 'but only for a short time. He's doing the rounds before he takes over from his father as president and publisher.'

I said: 'How nice!'

Finally, it was time to say farewell, although John said it

would form a perfect finish if I could return that night to watch how the newspaper was going to cover the results of the elections which had taken place that day. We agreed to wait on the weather. In the meantime, he took me in his car to catch the bus at a point from where he collected me each day. But as usual, the bus didn't seem to be coming according to schedule. So we got out of the cold air and of our damp overcoats into the warmth of a coffee shop by the road side. John ordered cups for us two, and there in the smoky shop we complimented ourselves for a good meeting, adding in the process more smoke clouds from our lungs to that already floating in the room. Feeling at that moment more than close to the man, I pointed to a block of buildings overlooking the place. A lot of black folks seemed to come in and out of there.

'Are there many coloured people in New Brunswick?' I asked.

'Oh, quite a number.'

'And how are they?'

'We are doing a lot for them,' John said warmly. 'Why, look at the new blocks by the river. You ought to come again so I can take you to see them. *The Home News* did a lot of fighting to have the development of the place carried out by the city council. Oh, it should ease the Negro lot a great deal, and there is more we want to do for them.'

I felt the coffee turn clayish on my tongue. Poor blacks, I contained my thoughts, they don't even form part of their own society. Like children or aliens, things usually are done for them. Whenever the adults and patrons are so willing and in the mood to be generous, then a little gift or concession here and there for these helpless and powerless. I did not want to prick the expansive balloon or bubble of my fine host, so climbing down the tall stool I sat on, I spotted the bus just then pulling to a stop outside in the drift, and said as sincerely as I could: 'Goodbye old fellow, and thanks for everything.'

There was a comic epilogue to my *Home News* visit. Several days after, I got a letter from John. Part of it was the house magazine of some alumni association somewhere in the State of New Jersey. It carried a lead story captioned 'Letter from Lagos' as sent home by one of their far-ranging members, a Jesuit father. And there on the cover, as large as life, against a map of Western Nigeria, was a white-over-black photograph of its author, in all the habits and humility of his order, telling the story of that unending mission to bring light to yet another dark people.

The Washington Post after *The Home News*, was like going from a shop in New York's lower east side to a departmental store like Lord and Taylor on Fifth Avenue. Of course the smooth, endless machinery appears the same, the same material is mixed and served to a mass public, and the men are the same ants all over again, walking over one another in the rush and push to make the grade. Only the display of wares shows louder, the size of market larger, and the managers get more and more involved with the business of creating and directing tastes and fashion both at home and abroad. This is more so with *The Washington Post*, as the paper tries to do what even the *New York Times* in all its volumes and verbiage still sees as a fond hope – serving as the national newspaper of a country that is really a continent.

A strange club of several disparate members, each with his own rash of communication organs to preach, represent, and uphold the dignity and inalienable rights of every American, that is, the property owner – the Union that Lincoln saved still lacks one such common institution as found in smaller and more compact countries. So publishing in the federal capital where the president of the club, with all the cohorts of chucker-outs at his command, is bravely doing his best to defend and protect a constitution about which no two members of the club agree, *The Washington Post* assumes a role and a tone, that, one may venture to say at this safe distance, are not altogether in keeping with the paper's actual stature and performance. My visit to that establishment therefore proved more than just an advance from the relatively pioneering business at home to the limitless confines and resources of a corporation; my journey there became something of a pilgrimage and I was glad when it was over.

Lunch, after a dizzy tour of the place conducted by a young reporter, who said he was doing research into the communication methods and habits of the Ibo people in Nigeria, was a high-powered affair, in one of those gleaming dining-rooms that together with a complete kitchen service form a healthy appendage of every American establishment worthy to be called a corporation. The managing editor, Mr Alfred Friendly, a most friendly host, took me up and introduced me to his colleagues, a whole circle of them. Their names and positions soon ceased to matter in the clatter of silver and tabletalk. At the head of table sat a distinguished gentleman who I thought was the great Phil Graham himself, owner by marriage and more of the establishment. Beginning with him, flanked on one side by a young lady staff member and on the other by the day's guest, who happened to be me, and going up to the managing editor at the other end of the table, and then finally to the rest of the exclusive group filling in both sides, all of this apparently according to some pre-ordained arrangement, the black anonymous housekeeper served us hot toasted grape fruit, followed this with the main dish of steak and something, offered dessert which I declined, and finally rich black coffee of which everybody took a generous helping. It was quite a ritual, with a rising cross-current of dialogue and chorus to it, with she alone, the one that mattered, playing a dump part.

Earlier, in the elevator going up, I had started what turned out to be a proper prologue.

'I have a letter for the editor,' I said.

'Oh, have you? And where is it?' Mr Friendly asked in his

warm baritone voice, crushing like gravel in a barrel rolling
down a road.

'I still have to write it!' I laughed.

'Please do, but what on?'

'You carried a news-story about Nigeria on your main
features page yesterday.'

'Oh yes, about the emergency situation up there in the
Western State.'

'Western Region,' I began.

'Oh, yes, Western Region of Nigeria. Very interesting
development that.'

'Yes, but it's six months' old.'

'Really? What about the treason trials?'

'Those have just come up and take barely a couple of
paragraphs in your story, which I must say you gave a good
amount of space.'

'Well, we are trying the best we can to cover Africa.'

'You mean the Congo Republic and Algeria, and perhaps
Nasser and Nkrumah –'

'Well, we are doing the best we can. That story you spoke
of, for instance, was filed by our own man in West Africa
stationed at Dakar. He's a very well-known correspondent.'

'Undoubtedly!' I agreed. 'I remember the fellow was
thrown out of Ghana and some other place.'

At this point, a curtain of silence fell between, which did
not lift until we were inside and had fallen on the fare.

'Mr Clark, what did you think of the Cuban crisis?'

'Think?' I looked up. So sudden had come the question and
such was the short-circuit way it charged the room, for a
time I paused palpably between the food going at that
moment into my mouth and the words that everybody had
stopped and was waiting to hear come out of there.

'Think?' I repeated. 'But was there room to think?'

'Oh, come come,' gurgled the distinguished gentleman at
the head of the table, for it was he who had popped the
question on me. 'Surely,' he went on, 'you must have

reacted in some way. Why, the world was on the very brink of total nuclear war in those first days when Russian ships kept steaming towards the cordon of quarantine the US had thrown about Cuba. Don't tell me you slept through it all.'

'Well, surprising as it may seem,' I began, finding passage at last for words and food, 'I slept quite soundly in the thick of the crisis.'

'How was that?' several voices spouted.

'Oh, simple. I never for one moment believed Kennedy and Kruschev would actually blow themselves up. Both men are too proud of their western civilization and its great achievements to want to blow it up.'

Return of silver to plates and the shift of chairs forward and back provided the only sound of life for a good number of seconds. And I think Mr Friendly in his warm open voice growled something about that being a swell thought to go to bed on, although it turned out none would let the matter lie there.

'But what did you think of the US at that time? Did you think the President had done right declaring the quarantine?' urged my distinguished host who, I came to know, was Mr Wiggins, the editorial page boss.

'Remember, those missiles in Cuba meant the Reds were within a striking reach of Washington, New York, and even Chicago and San Francisco,' another, the man to my right, added.

'But you forget you have bases encircling Russia all the way from Iceland to Okinawa,' I ventured to point out.

'Nonsense, those have been there all along.' Someone snorted across the table.

'Cuba was just one against scores,' I insisted.

'That one base, as you put it, completely upset the balance of power against the Free World.'

'Hence it was worth taking the risk of war involving all the world?'

'That's a good question,' Mr Wiggins laughed, taking the

steam off the air which by now was quite missile-charged.

'I think Phil Graham asked the President just that one question, didn't he, Alf?'

'Yes, but will anyone ever know the true answer?' Alf Friendly gave a half laugh. And to that note of self-questioning the party broke up.

Some weeks after, I wrote what you may call an epilogue to that *Washington Post* drama, and its theme was that terrible shadow-boxing game both the United States and the Soviet Union engaged everybody in over the close ring of Cuba. It goes like this:

> With my hammer head
> I'll smash up the earth,
> Said
> The lizard:
> And up reared
> The aroused crown,
> And then down
> The blow
> Came – like a courtesan's head,
> Deep in her pillow.

There were a couple more episodes. On my second day at the house, after listening in at the editorial conference, a most judicial affair with India's Nehru under close examination in the matter of brutal assault at the hands of Chinese thugs, I was handed over to Mr Karl Meyer, a young editorial writer who revealed to me he also writes for the *New Statesman*. Because of an earlier lunch engagement, he passed me on to a colleague in the news section who in turn asked me to meet another co-worker so we could all go together for lunch in some joint around the corner. 'Take care of him' had been Mr Meyer's parting words. 'He's a journalist from Nigeria, and from what I hear, a writer of some considerable talent.'

I never had that lunch, for once inside the restaurant, my two new friends and I got into an argument over neutrality, morals and all that.

'What are the feelings in Nigeria over China's invasion of India?' one of them pinned me down even as we sank into our seats. I said I didn't quite know, having been away from home for some time, and that my own brother was right then serving as a diplomat in India; and I said something to the effect that India and Nigeria were both Commonwealth nations, that Nigerian soldiers fought in India and Burma to keep out the Japs, and that naturally her sympathy must go to India, especially as China appeared the aggressor.

'That's all well and good,' the man said, 'but it doesn't alter the fact that that man Nehru is an ass.'

'What a stupid thing to say,' I started. 'A senator of yours said the same thing on TV the other day –'

'Yes, and very right he was. Nehru for a long time has been riding the high horse of neutrality and all that. Now that he has been hit hard by the Reds, he wants help from the US. Let the so-called neutrals save India with their morals.'

'Is Nehru an ass because he has no H-bombs to defend his neutral position? Tell me, is that what makes his morals nonsense?'

'For a long time he has been preaching that only the yellows and blacks of the world have the right to morality and judgment. Now they are fighting themselves and want the awful white man to step in.' By this time we were fairly shouting at each other, so that the proprietor, anxious for his other customers all of whom were looking curiously at us, came over to our table and asked if we cared for anything.

'I want nothing to eat,' I said.

'There, are you afraid we'll poison you?' my host laughed from the left corner of his mouth.

'Nonsense,' I spat out, 'if you think I'm going to die on this side of the Atlantic, you are mistaken.'

'He's taken our drink, anyway,' the other baited.

'Yes,' I agreed. 'And that's real foreign aid offered to the wrong man, isn't it?'

Then there was that hop to some shopping centre I took with one well-seasoned newshen on the eve of that great holiday of the Americans – Thanksgiving Day. We stopped for quite a while to talk to the manager of the big super-market which, together with the bowling alleys close by formed the nerve-centre of what otherwise consisted of heaps of broken bones and bottles that once supported houses, and freshly patched up flesh and skin that passed for the new structures and superior positions fashionably styled urban renewal.

How many families affected? How many again on their feet? And with what amount of room to move about? Yes, compensations there must be, but are the brass and tin limbs provided really a replacement for the so-called withered ones amputated? For all these questions my female escort promised to furnish me adequate answers. Only I should wait until we got back to the office, for it was the *Washington Post*, more than any other force, that had moved the city authorities to embark on this project of rehousing Washington's hard-pressed lower-income groups. And these just happen to be Negro. They squat in the city centre, while those with money have beautiful homes out in the open greens of the suburbs, making the capital look like a dough-nut, all blighted and hollow inside.

'Do you miss talking over the hedge to your neighbour?' my newshen stopped an old woman sorting out what provisions to buy herself.

'I don't know what you mean,' the old woman said. 'All I know is they've moved me from my home, and now I'm in this new hole in their big, mountain, apartment block. I may as well be in a home – in an institution for the old. Now that's what they should call the place. Only the kids are so many, playing football down the street. I suppose the young folks like it, but me, I'm seventy, so nothing don't matter.'

'Pleasant thoughts for eve of Thanksgiving Day,' I said. 'You bet,' the newshen cackled, moving us on in search for better grounds to scratch.

Back in the office and safe in the hands of Mr Friendly I asked if I could tag along with the man standing for the *Washington Post* at the President's news conference that night.

'Impossible,' he dismissed the idea. 'That's for working editors only, and there's absolutely nothing I can do to help.'

'Well, thanks all the same, for everything. As for that news conference I'll make sure I see it on TV.'

'Yes, that's where I shall watch it too,' he shook my hands.

'Thanks again and enjoy your trip to Europe.'

'I sure will try to, although it is a working trip,' he said filling the doorway, and 'do come again.'

I should have taken advantage of that offer, mere formula though I had come to recognize it. There were others in the *Washington Post* family I very much wanted to cultivate their acquaintance, namely, the magazine *Newsweek*, and the TV and sound network of the American Broadcasting Company, both of them, it goes without saying, very important and influential bodies in their own right.

3 · THE BLACKS

'The Negro baby born in America today, regard-
less of the section or the state in which he is born,
has about one-half as much chances of completing
high school as a white baby, born in the same place,
on the same day; one third as much chance of
becoming a professional man; twice as much chance
of becoming unemployed; about one-seventh as
much chance of earning $10,000 a year; a life
expectancy which is seven years shorter and the
prospects of earning only half as much.'

PRESIDENT JOHN KENNEDY.

On TV again was James Meredith, this time at the end of
his first term at Oxford, Mississippi. His term report was
none too good, in fact it might lead to his being sent down.
It was not read and given to the public by his tutors but by a
co-ed doing the same year and course with the problem
student. And how had she come by her facts? Oh, he simply
wasn't asking questions any more in class. Rings show around
his eyes, and he yawns and fidgets, during lectures. Sad,
wasn't it, this whole affair? It was a most remarkable

performance by this young lady on a live and nation-wide broadcast. Hands over notebook on a neutral lap, her back erect, and hair swept modishly behind in a mauve scarf, there she sat facing the cameras and all the world, not afraid to show her face, and not worried about giving her name. Only one or two interviews before, boys and girls, the very scions of the old Southern stock that has to be saved from pollution, in discussing this same Negro James Meredith and his forced grafting and entry into their midst, had worn hoods and masks and would not reveal their identity for fear of violence or worse being done to them by friends and compatriots to whom the very name of the intruder was anathema and incitement to fury and folly. Not that her account exactly made her out as an angel in the cause of peace and respect from one man to another, however shady in colour, but in the face of so much devilry and foolishness as was around, it was easy to forget to ask why one of America's three largest TV networks should choose to have one student report upon another, why they failed to recognize that with the unbelievable strain and circumstances under which the man already was working, it was sheer absurd craze for pain and mischief to submit him to further pressure and treatment of this type, and what exactly were the poor marks he had earned that placed him so poorly beside other students at Ole Miss, bright and backward together.

That however was not the end of the sensational reporting. James Meredith himself was soon put on view. Close-cropped, jacket flailing in the wind, and arms full of a couple of paper boxes, he walked up to his car parked close by, let himself in through a door still showing dented and battered by bricks and bottles that were part of the warm welcome he had had only months before. And now, coming into view, as if to make sure no zealot came up and clobbered their ward from behind, were the US marshals and guards that kept a close and constant watch over James Meredith, the Negro, investing him with the singular but double honour of being the only one of his race to register in the University of Mississippi and the one student and citizen anywhere in the world enjoying a personal guard larger and stronger than that of his president or king.

Apparently, there had been no sign his troubles would come to an end. Admission had come to him at the point of a bayonet and there had even been bloodshed when federal troops returned fire in a desperate effort to quell a riot of gown and town. And latest of all, some unrelenting vigilantes, under cover of dark, had shot at his father's home. Was there point then in carrying on the crusade, especially as he appeared a lonely black knight, with no new champions and fresh recruits flocking to the flag? Undoubtedly, this was the agony of the man, and it was to find resolution with himself that he was now going home to his wife and parents. Had the man then actually cracked up? Or would he come back? As Attorney-General Bobby Kennedy said on behalf of his brother, himself and all liberal and law-abiding US citizens, the damage from a retreat like that would prove irreparable and deep. After this, to pursue the charge of contempt of court against Governor Barnett, a course of action already too politically awkward to press home with advantage, would be like prosecuting the unscrupulous executor of an estate for trying to keep an heir out of his birthright and title when the young man has already dispossessed himself.

The strange mixture of carefree laughter and embarrassed silence that was the student response in Princeton's Graduate College to the sick conditions of their country, was rankling still in my ears, when my hostess for that evening drove in to take me home to a party she and her husband were giving for a small circle of friends. Princeton was snow-bound then, so that we skidded in the huge station-wagon as we pulled out. She ought to have taken me on my word, she said, and let me come over in a taxicab as I had offered to do. Her doctor husband was out late in the hospital putting his patients away for the night, but he should be home by the time we got there. It's your society, I thought to myself, that needs the doctor's care, for it is sadly sick at heart. What with that state of mind myself, the party was for me no huge success. The children of the house wanted a carol or two before they would go off to bed, so we crowded round their mother who told us what tunes to sing by playing their first bars on the piano, but whether it was the raw weather outside or the sheer scientific weight of the guests inside, carols that should be familiar and clear in a Christian country came out broken and indifferent. Little wonder that the children, not quite impressed and satisfied, kept asking for yet another, like Oliver Twist. But soon they were bundled off to bed so the older folks could have their fun undisturbed.

Whatever fun there was at the party flickered like the fire in the hearth, and one spurt of tongue that comes vividly to mind was of a medical man. 'Those are tribal marks on your face?' He lit up suddenly.

'Not exactly,' I laughed.

'How do you mean, not exactly? They must be; they look like tribal marks to me.'

'And what may those be?'

'Oh, surely, you must know – to tell you from fellows of an enemy tribe.'

'Perhaps so, but mine don't fall into your classification.'

'What are they then?'

'Innoculation or vaccination marks, I should say.'

'Now young man, you are kidding.'

'No, I'm not.'

'You mean some herb was rubbed as antidote into those marks when they were made? By the way, who was it made them? A medicine-man? And did he actually cut you with some knife not sterilized at all, and you wide awake?'

'There, there, you two,' our kind hostess came between us, 'are you two still teasing each other?'

At that, both of us protested, at the same time, and with these same words: 'Of course, I am not teasing!' After which, we let ourselves be led apart and helped separately to more drinks or food, but such was the attraction of the subject to us both, like a pair of tongs stuck at the middle, that several times we sought each other out, although never quite meeting, in vain fitful efforts to probe what must have appeared to his scientific mind a sore as it was to me a dying fire.

On the way home I asked to be dropped. The young couple who had offered me the ride would not hear of it.

'We will take you right up to the Graduate College,' they extended their offer, 'Don't you see it's so cold? And the hour is late, you know. There can't be anything on in Princeton at this time of night.' They really were anxious for me, but seeing they had a stubborn fellow to deal with, let me out into the night, and probably were somewhat relieved to see me blend so well with it. The young professor of mathematics or something had got out from behind his driver's seat and held the door of the car open for me to come out. Now as he climbed back behind the wheel I heard him shout over his shoulders and the roof of the car: 'Hey, man, give her a good screwing!'

'What's that?' I turned round although I had heard him all right. In the cold and dark there with snow beginning to flake again I was rather unprepared for the sudden thawing and loosening of tongue in a fellow guest who all night in the warmth and brightness of a close party had refused to touch any cocktail, draining cup after cup of black coffee when he was not helping his wife to some of the inebriating fare lying half taken in the self-service set up. So it was more in mischief than misunderstanding that I had thrown my question, although this did not quite throw him out of his new gear.

'I said give the black beauty a good fucking,' the man fumbled for his keys.

'You didn't hear what my husband said, did you?' his wife assured me over and across his back. I noticed she was actually holding the man down.

'No, of course, I didn't. That's why I asked,' I said.

'Well, John was wondering if you shouldn't come over and have a drink with us,' she smiled.

'I said nothing of the sort,' John grunted. 'You know there is no drink in the house.'

'Darling, don't be silly! Of course there's beer left in the ice-box.'

'But I drank it all up before we set out for the party,' he chuckled.

'No!' the woman glared. 'When was that?'

'Well good night,' I waved to them, not wanting to be exposed further to the heat of some family brawl.

'Yes, good night then,' the young woman barely smiled, and then to her husband who was again telling me to make sure I had a good time: 'Stop fumbling, John! Don't you see you left the engine running all the time?'

And so under the lash and steam of her tongue, they drove off at last, the man still chuckling to himself and the car coughing and careering dangerously down the frozen road and into the cold and dark of the night.

Hard luck for me, it was no lover maid, black beauty or blonde, that I went to wake up that night. One side-street into another brought me to the door of a house half-hidden in front by shadowy elm trees flecked with snow. My fingers were numb, so I must have knocked at the door louder than was necessary. A man opened it just wide enough for him to block the passage, but with a brusque 'hi' greeting, which brought between the man and me a thick screen of smoke from my lungs, I brushed past him and several other persons, straight into the bar and lounge, and because the cold and wetness in my shoes were at this point two thorny shoots growing into me, I kicked free my boots and peeled off my overcoat and gloves before coming to a stop at the bar. 'Hey' the man who had let me in called out to everybody there, 'never met this brother before!' Nor it seemed had the other brothers and daughters of the place, for they all regarded me in silence, their eyes shifting between my face and the glasses

arrested empty or half-way in their hands. I felt like the
Iceman himself. Until the girl at the bar looked past the
customers who hugged her all round and cried out in real
surprise and joy: 'Hey, man, where hev you been?'

'Been seeing more of your country,' I laughed back. 'And
how are you, Becky? You look great.'

'Really?' she beamed, not putting a finger wrong on her
cash machine which she kept at a steady run. At that, somebody from among the brothers and daughters there gathered,
said: 'She ought to thank the good Lord for that.'

'Oh, now,' another tossed down a drink. 'It's herself she
should thank. Why, Becky's got enough mouths to make a
cow's teat turn rags. But there she's still with a figure to
light the fire in a man's heart.'

'There, you haven't told me that before!' Becky laughed.

'His missus at home don't let him do any such thing. She
got the big stick!' someone said.

'Oh, let her lie,' Sam rubbed his palm and smacked his lips,
'I do what I have mind to.'

'Like pinch girls on their backsides?'

'You shut your trap, will you? I should've brought her
roses long time before, a bunch of them bigger than any
you'll ever get from the undertaker. But fellows like you will
stick out their tongues.'

'Now, now, aren't you shooting your mouth wide? As if
your fires can be stoked up anymore than by striking match
on snow.'

'Maybe it's yours that burn no more,' Sam sucked his
teeth. Then turning his hunched-up back on everybody there,
he reached out his glass and said: 'Some poison please,
Becky, my sweet.'

I got myself a drink too and settled on a very high stool
against the counter. At my elbow was a young man who said
he had met me before, the first time I came in there with some
friends of mine. One of them, he said, was from Yugoslavia,
wasn't he? 'Hey, man,' my new found friend nudged me in

the ribs, 'Isn't that country behind the Iron Curtain?'

'Rather astride it,' I said.

'Funny, that.' He scratched his close-cropped head. 'How come you moving with fellows like that?' I laughed, but before I could get in a word, he shifted on his seat and so on to another matter entirely.

'Hey, honey,' he motioned to Becky, 'let that drink be on me. No, no,' he brushed off my half-hearted protests. 'You come from Africa, don't you?'

'That's right,' I said.

'Then we are brothers,' he announced. I took his offer and there in the glare of eyes stronger than all the neon-lights dancing in the mist of the place I ventured to ask whether he was a Black Moslem.

'I ain't nothing of the sort,' he stayed me with one hand as the other ferreted in his overcoat pocket for loose dollar bills and change to pay for the beer he was standing me his brother from Africa. 'No, I ain't nothing like what you call a Black Moslem' he underlined his point. 'I do my job at the post office and when I feel like it, I come over here for my scotch and soda.'

'That's right,' said Sam from the corner into which he had sunk. 'That's right, son. A man's got no right not to serve you a pint some, after a day in yonder salt mines. Now, look here, honey, pour me out the poison. Will you?'

'I knew we were heading for that.' A daughter kicked the counter. Everybody laughed.

'I don't need no excuse to have me booze,' Sam dismissed it all.

Somebody had put another dime or quarter in the juke-box, and now a big raucous voice was belting away at a number which instantly got everyone there clapping and swaying on their seats. A few even joined in the singing, swinging to the beat, snapping their fingers at no one in particular, and before long, they were shouting, eyes shut tight, as lustily as the local star in the slot, only being much more bodily there, their combined voice filled out the place more than the smoke cloud from their cigarettes.

'Not so loud, folks,' Becky appealed to them.

'Hell,' one said 'is there a damned place a man can blow his top without some kind of cop showing up?'

'What do you want to blow your top for anyway?' Sam smirked, 'When the goddam bottom of it stays solid from the light of day?'

'Those of the Black Moslems don't like such music, nor drink,' I said, again very tactless. 'They say both make you sleep.'

'You pity us very much, don't you?' the young man who had bought me a drink pinned me down.

'Why do you say that?' I asked.

'He should hev a long time ago, young man,' an elderly woman came in. 'I been hearing all that's said here this night, and don't you go away thinking I don't. We brothers and daughters meet here as one family. But it don't look you like our ways, least of all, our drinking and singing habits.' I made to say something but there again was Sam.

'Don't say nothing,' he raised his balmy palm. 'Every sinner got a right to get boozed before the moon turns round. Don't they in Africa – or ain't that the country you from?'

I said yes. 'Then, let's drink all together as one family,' he held up my hand. 'None of us, not with all the blessed Indian and African tribes behind us, can push the Kennedys off their high seat, can we?'

'Why not?' I asked.

'There he goes!' someone said in disgust. 'The fellow's come from Africa to do our fighting for us.'

Fortunately, there was no fighting that night. Some more money had gone into the music box, and the very first disc to fall into place, a twister, whipped quite a few couples there up on their feet. The gentleman, who had earlier let me in, came up to me, with a cigarette burning close and dangling dangerously between his lips. He was something like the floor-manager of the place and now wanted me to join in the dance and forget my argumentative ways.

'I don't know how to dance,' I said.

'You – an African? you kidding.'

'Sincerely, I don't.'

'Oh, you just feeling superior or what?'

'Shy, maybe,' a woman laughed. 'Oh, I know these fighting men.'

'Come, I'll show you,' the floor manager offered, and more ash fell off his cigarette on both our fronts. 'It isn't hard at all. Well, brother, do you smoke?' I said no, that I used to be a three-pack-a-day man. At which he said I certainly must have terrific will-power, and when I protested it was nothing to do with will-power, that on the contrary the taste of a cigarette had stopped my smoking it after a bad cold two years back, he said: 'Never mind, brother. What matters is that you still can put out a fag under your foot, or can't you?' So saying he dropped the stump burning closer still between his lips and asked me to stub it out on the floor. I did his command and he was lavish with commendation for me.

'Now, what did I tell you? You can dance as well as any of us. It's just boiling in the blood of us black people. You just keep moving like you're putting that cigarette out all your life – Yes, that's all the motion, man, and you see, the pretty baby is all yours!'

Back in my rooms, because I still was wide-eyed and rest-less and unable to read, I tried to clear the backlog of my mail. But it was useless; the only letter I began and addressed to my brother in India, I finished several days after. And when sleep came at last, it turned out to be one nightmare featuring my brother and James Meredith all mixed up in one terrible role and struggle for identity and survival, a nightmare short but self-repeating and more live than anything I remember on screen or stage. So that all I did on waking up shaky from bed was put the seal of my hand on the brand new piece that

had forged itself in the automatic boiler of my subconscious
even while I slept:

> Last night, times out of dream,
> I woke
> To the sight of a snake ·
> Slithering in the field, livid
> Where the grass is
> Patched, merged up where it runs
> All shades of green – and suddenly!
> My brother in India, up, stick
> In hand, poised to strike –
> But ah, himself is struck
> By this serpent, so swift,
> So silent, with more reaction
> Than a nuclear charge . . .
>
> And now this morning with eyes still
> To the door, in thought of a neck
> Straining under the sill,
> I wake
> To the touch of a hand as
> Mortal and fair, asking
> To be kissed, and a return
> To bed, my brothers
> In the wild of America!

My first real encounter with the American Negro was in
New York a week or so after my arrival in the country, and
it took the form of a reunion with a girl from Columbia who
had only then recently returned home from doing research
work in Nigeria. I had wired her to come over and fetch me
at my lodgings down in Greenwich Village, since her family
was not listed on the telephone book and I was still like a
sleep-walker in the city. We missed each other the first time
she called. I had gone out with my host in search of two young

girls who had called for him while he was out and had left
word behind with me that they were off to do some early
skating at Madison Square Gardens and that they wanted to
be picked up when the fun was over.

'Were they fun?' Gloria asked.

'Rather,' I said. 'Teenagers you know – one said she was
at the City College and the other is a secretary in some firm
although she says she's training at the same time to record
proceedings for a judge.'

'Does that mean you couldn't sleep with any of them, or
isn't that always your aim with every pretty skirt you run
into?'

'My host danced his partner into the kitchen and claims
they made love there and then.'

'And you?'

'Oh, I tried to with the other who was drinking on the sofa
with me – a real kitten of a girl.'

'Did you have her? Oh, I see, you've begun mincing words.'

'Well, she was rather mixed up,' I said. 'Even like the
blood in her veins which she said was part African, part
Spanish, part Red Indian, and I think, part Mongolian, but
she's Negro all right, she told me.'

'All of which amounts to a defeat?'

'Yes, if you like putting it that way. What can you do
with a hedge-hog when it bundles itself up into a pad tighter
than all adhesives?' She had got up on her feet, and finishing
a sort of pivot, faced me and asked in her direct way: 'How do
you like my hair-do?'

'I preferred your hair as it was – natural.'

'But what can I do?' she broke out. 'You know in Nigeria I
wore it that way. But even there I was thought a schoolgirl.
All grown-ups in the cities, I found, wear it straight. And
out here of course they think you are crazy or just putting on
an act if you don't.'

'Yes, so I see. Even the men.'

'Oh, isn't that really horrible, men wearing curlers and

reeking with oil. But that's what years of slavery have done to us as a people – we imitate the white in everything – even to the point of wanting to bleach our skin.'

She had begun walking up and down the floor and now I could see she was wearing those long nylon stockings and sharp high-heeled shoes. 'You don't like them,' she caught my eyes.

'I said nothing of the sort.'

'Oh, come off it,' she said. 'Don't tell me you already have fallen a victim of the systematic brainwashing. You see I am wearing my hair long and glossy, and on my skin shines the special cream I must rub on it if I am not to appear leprous. Do you know the hot stretching-comb was actually invented in a farm down South for the black women whom their white masters desired and possessed by force? Well, have they got their hands on you too, and so early?'

'Who knows?' I said. 'You ought to see the verse I have written since coming over. Maybe, your expert eye will detect the change there.'

'Oh, you've been writing? That's very good. Once or twice I have been worried that I pressured you to come, fearing that like Dylan Thomas, it might affect you for the worse.'

'I hope not!' I laughed.

'And are you thinking of publishing? What about your play – any plans for staging it yet?'

I said some Madison Avenue friends had suggested Mr Langston Hughes should get together a Negro cast but that I had shocked them by asking why the production had to be black when my play was simply for human beings everywhere and about human beings who happened to be in one particular place and situation.

'Oh, you ought to let them!' she clasped her hands. 'But then, you'll forget us now you are moving in the upper brackets.'

'Don't be silly, Gloria!'

'I am not; you actually asked me at home why you should be bothering yourself with the blacks in America when the whites would love you to death?'

'Good Lord,' I held her by the shoulders, 'You are even more of a masochist than me.'

'Rubbish,' she said and plumped back on her seat. But she was up again immediately, saying we must be out and hurrying if she was to see some professor at her college at a particular hour, and if we were both going to have lunch together, or didn't I want to tour Harlem with her? I jumped at that multiple invitation and on our way, asked how she was feeling now she was home again.

'I can't tell exactly,' she said. 'In Africa I felt at home, much more so I thought than I could remember in all my life. But then there was my mother as well as my brothers, you will see them before you go. Naturally I wanted to be back among them, especially Sister, that's my mother, as we all call her. And of course, there is my thesis to finish. Anyway, now I am back, I don't exactly know where I belong. Perhaps I'll go back to Nigeria or some other place in Africa, I don't really know.'

Except for the professor part of it, the programme she had arranged came off without a hitch. We even picked up some warm clothing for me to wear in the colder days ahead, an exercise taken as we got out of Columbia into Harlem, and which spread quite a conscientious glow in both my friend and me as that had been my one ostensible reason for being out of Princeton at that time of week.

But best of all, Gloria took me home out on the Bronx, and so it was I got within the orbit and glow of that amazing phenomenon, so retiring and never quite acknowledged and yet providing the major, if not the entire, source of light in the heart-breaking, bleak confines of the Negro in America, I mean, the matriarch. Gloria's mother had been away all day at work and now she arrived large, beautiful and shedding warmth and care all over the house.

'Aren't you freezing, children?' she asked. 'I see, that window there is wide open. And how are you feeling, child? Gloria told us you'd come to see us sometime. Has she given you something to eat? No, I guess not!' she said half smiling, half scolding. And all along, she suited action to her words, pulling into place the open window, coming back across the floor to give her daughter's friend a closer look, and that done, she allowed Gloria to help her put down the big paperbag bulging under her arm.

'What have you been buying, sister? You see, JP? I told him I couldn't tell what sweet things you'll be bringing home with you.'

'That's no good reason for keeping the boy hungry,' Sister said, taking off her great coat.

'I haven't really felt hungry,' I laughed. 'We have been drinking and talking, although I'm dying to see Gloria cook.'

'You mean I don't know how to – Sister, do you hear that?'

'Oh, you go off and take them straight to the kitchen. And what would you like to eat?' she turned to me. 'Something hot and with pepper?'

'Oh, cook us some rice, won't you, Sister?' Gloria stopped half-way between the sitting-room and kitchen.

'Oh, so it's Sister going to cook after all!' I laughed.

'Mind her?' Sister winked at me. 'Now, my boy, there is some beef and fish in the house, and I think some pork. Which will you have and what kind of stew do you like with it?'

'Any,' I jumped in my seat. 'Do you know, Sister, all the rice I've eaten so far has been dry, I mean without stew?'

'Yes, he says he's had no cooked meal since coming these two weeks,' Gloria chipped in.

'Poor boy,' her mother looked me over again. 'You must be starving and here we stand talking and doing nothing.' And she was out immediately in the passage, almost tripping over Prince, the dog and pet of the family. 'Oh, Prince, you

stop it.' She fondled the big brown creature that very often
was her one companion in the house. 'Taken him for his walk
yet, Gloria? No? You should, you know. That boy who
helps me isn't coming for another week.'

So getting back into our overcoats and mufflers, Gloria
and I took out Prince for a walk in the early and chilling
night. We did quite some distance among the plots, each
rising around us shadowy and high like a range of hills with
flanks broken here and there by light as from fires in a
thousand cells and caves. Altogether it was quite an experience. Prince was on the leash and Gloria and I were
supposed to be leading him so he could relieve himself, but
all along, in point of fact, it was the dog that did the leading
and we the following. Prince went where his nose took him,
down the kerb, across streets, in between and out of the cars
parked for the night in endless lines at street-sides, and
whatever pace we took, trotting or just dawdling, was as
Prince's legs and fancy said we should. Just one side of the
exercise we had control of, the conversation we kept running
all through the walk, and in that Prince had little or no
interest.

Sister had finished cooking and laid the table, but she was
wearing her apron still and watching TV when Prince, Gloria
and I returned to the apartment. She didn't rise to meet us
but then there was hardly any need for that as her presence
filled the place to overflowing. There she sat, the archetypal
image of mother and mourner as well as guardian and co-
sufferer of every member of her embattled race. For hundreds
of years, in a land of equal opportunity and freedom she has
kept watch, wept and waited; as all her sons were forced out
into the fields to labour for others to reap the abundant fruit,
and for this flogging and worse misfortune has been their
wages; as her brothers were hurled out of the house to be
hanged from trees or stoned to death without trial for
offences as little or non-existent as asking for their birthright
or casting an innocent eye on a harlot who happened to be

white; as her daughters, desired and defiled by lustful masters, were made to bear a bastard breed and then turned out to walk the streets, and she has watched and waited in vain when her husband that should be the pillar and prop of the house has broken under the burden and taken after to poisoned drinking, to beating and cursing everybody all day long and then finally walked out into the dark, never to return or be heard from. And in all this deprivation and abasement of her seed she has sought out of odd ends and scattered bits to keep together the broken structure of her family, and in several instances succeeded beyond all miracle through a sheer incapacity to fail and be crushed.

'How long you've been!' Sister greeted us, and so awoke me out of my momentary dream of her.

'Prince took a long time coming to the point,' Gloria grumbled.

'Oh, he missed you all this time you have been away at college – you in Africa, my small one in Carolina and your elder brother now out of the army and driving a bus on Long Island. But come, children, come into the kitchen. Or would you rather eat here and watch TV? Not that there's anything special going except for a funny fellow making faces at every person and thing.' We elected for the kitchen and there she led us. She had the food warming in the oven and she went up there straight to serve it.

'Aren't you joining us, Sister?' Gloria asked.

'No, you go on eating; I had a sandwich at the works.'

'Where's that?' I asked above the huge heap steaming in my front.

'Oh, mother works in some Jewish laundry plant out in the city,' Gloria said. 'You know the joke here in New York? The Jews provide the business and the Negroes the labour.'

'You go on eating your food,' Sister admonished good-humouredly. 'And don't lead the boy into talking. You'll both get your food in the wrong pipe.'

The food went down the proper way all right and afterwards we retired to a good night's rest half way or so through the Late Show. Very early the next morning, from the big couch in the sitting-room which had been sprung into a double-bed for me, I heard Sister telling a still slumbering Gloria about the breakfast she had already in the kitchen for us children, and then wrapped in her winter clothes and holding a big bag, Sister let herself out for another long day at work for the benefit of her brood.

Of the large body of professionals, artists, and intellectuals whose shady colouring assigns them to a sort of limbo in the American hierarchy, I saw very little to win me over from the unsparing views of the late Professor Frazier in his 'Black Bourgeoisie', although much to enlist for them sympathy and understanding. Daubed in a white society as Negro lawyers, Negro doctors, Negro professors and Negro writers or entertainers, and therefore not quite belonging to the civilized and prosperous professional guilds and cults, this class of the blacks in America struck me as falling into two main groups. The first, much embarrassed that they stand out at all, would rather, like members of the middle class anywhere, that they were left alone to pursue their slow pension schemes in peace. When not worrying about the rent or mortgage on the house, or what brand of car to open new instalment payments on now the Jones have changed their own, and whether Jack Jnr. is smart enough to get into college and play football, they spend the little that is left of their time in pottering about, adding gadgets to the house, or better still, behind the closed doors of the club or fraternity lodge, safe away from wives who are for ever reminding them of the next rung to climb on the ladder of success. At house parties, they sit close by the bar, and especially if the hosts are white liberals and that kind, they conscientiously try to talk shop and swap stale jokes and wise-cracks carried over from another party no less wet and dreary, while all the time the women are together head to head like hens, scratching up this gossip about some neighbours out of hearing, or ruffling their own proud feathers and tempers with remembrance of gorgeous holidays past, and with hopes and plans of those still to come in some outlying state or far-off country in Europe and elsewhere:

'Oh, John and I took the family to California last time.'

'Yes, wasn't that real wonderful!'

'Everybody ought to do the United States from coast to coast.'

'And did you drive all the way?'

'Arthur made all of us fly, you know.'

'But, Sue, I still think a month or so in Europe is the best.'

Such often is the small talk engaging the entire mind of those of this special sub-class of negroes. All of which helps them like drug and drink to forget there is a strange destiny that has consigned their kind to a social limbo that neither touches the hell of the unemployed, uneducated and desperate of their race nor the heaven of the lowest of the whites to whose heights they aspire but cannot get assumption. Yet it is not uncommon to run into some, like the vivacious and formidable lady I met at a New Year party in Princeton, who when pricked briefly out of her cocoon and euphoria, swore something to the effect and in the hearing of her white hosts that whoever feels persecuted and oppressed under the sacred Constitution of the United States, the most democratic country on earth, deserves to remain so!

Members of the other sub-group, far from being faceless and forgetful of the garment of damnation in which America has for long invested the black in their midst, make a profession of their identity, and indeed a booming business out of it. Its members, like birds of the same feather, which in fact they are, very much move and associate in groups, societies and organizations. These sprout all over the land and are as diverse among themselves as one species of mushroom is edible and another fatal. Apparently, the one strain common to all these groups is their frenetic strife in one form or another to improve the lot of the black and make it possible for weed and wheat to survive together in the fabulous garden that is America. And they nearly all enjoy the backing of strong influential private donors, benefactors and foundations, several of them discreetly anonymous and not showing their hands. In fact, the patronage in some cases appears so lavish and guided that one or two uncharitable and ungrateful critics have spotted behind them some very muscular arm of state or corporate power with a great deal up its sleeves of lace and gold.

Typical and at once unique is the American Society for African Culture all very well set up in down-town New York. As is evident from its name, the society does not present a broad front in the fight to attain for the Negro an equal place, taken for granted in his native American society. Rather, the big point those in it make is the home they have found anew in Africa. Thus its sponsors, most of them Lincoln alumni, would shut out even those whites with genuine interest and perhaps better knowledge of Africa, a restriction and reverse bias that should stand the society in good stead if ever it comes out for sit-ins, freedom-rides, street demonstrations, and popular expressions of that kind, as the very respectable and gouty NAACP has had to do recently. But fortunately for AMSAC, it is always in better company and far removed from the bad breath and sweat of the man uptown in Harlem. Like some bored old lady with a lot of money and who is always scared to be alone by herself, the society is for ever thinking up some party or platform. And it has a nose that smells out an honoured guest from abroad even before he has set foot on US soil. Every leader of any delegation from Africa, preferably in sumptuous agbada or kente, is sedulously scouted out, courted and asked over by AMSAC to a party for which he pays with an address, often with only very little to do with culture except in the widest sense of the word. And of course no artist from Africa, on a grant the society knows little of or cares little about emulating, is ever missed on the list of notables the society constantly compiles to its credit, comfort and complacency.

In such circumstances, it matters very little if the religious and social significance of an original Bambara head-piece copied and proudly hung up on the wall of the AMSAC centre is completely lost and forgotten there. Perhaps it had not even been recognized to begin with. Indeed the mix-up and masquerade could be most crushing. The story goes that on one occasion the proud AMSAC host actually slapped on the back the honourable gentleman from Gabon and asked in great cheer how the old capital city of all the Congos was doing after that maverick Lumumba!

Most symptomatic of the social-climbing and status-seeking habits that probably provide the strongest driving force behind the AMSAC was that grand ball it gave last Christmas for all African ambassadors to the United Nations. Like the great festival of folly with which the society had earlier sought fame in Lagos, the gala affair featured luminaries and debutantes but gave little or no room to undiscovered stars and ordinary folks teeming in the ghettos of Harlem, perhaps for fear they might darken the gleaming hall and gates of the Hotel Americana. All was white ties and tails and mink stoles, and the fabulous Duke Ellington himself was there with his band to serenade everybody into dreamland. But not much dancing was done that night since everybody who was anybody or as likely as not part of that bleak stratum of society starved of high cocktail occasions, made sure of a place on the floor so as not to lose for another season or life this one chance of rubbing shoulders with the great of the land. With me that night was my friend James Ward, an old boy of Princeton only now beginning to put his weight behind the lever to upturn for once and all the oppressive burden his black people have had to bear all these many years. And between us sat in dazzling dress his old girl friend of schooldays in Philadelphia. They seemed quite overwhelmed with all the pomp and circumstance of the occasion, especially during the pompous roll-call of honoured guests present. First of them all, it turned out amid great cheers, was the distinguished US Ambassador to the UN, Mr Adlai Stevenson. The great man was even prevailed upon to make a speech and was walked to the rostrum by the super-host of the occasion Dr John A. Davis, all beaming and sweating with satisfaction. Later, when Duke struck up another tune well-remembered with tears by many, and when hosts and guests began shuffling on their feet and basking in all the limelight, Dr Davis and the partner in his arms stopped graciously in front of me.

'Meet my wife,' he said. We exchanged how-do-you-do, after which he kindly added: 'Have a dance with her.' I shook my head, and he asked why not. Without thought, I told him there and then I was disappointed in the whole show. Both husband and wife looked appropriately shocked, and appeared not to understand. So that in quick succession I asked: Why the build-up for the American Stevenson? How was it not one of his excellent friends from Africa had been given a similar opportunity of saying a word or two, or wasn't the party for them after all, but in fact for Ambassador Stevenson? And if he had to speak at all as the home representative, should that not be after the doyen among the African guests of honour had had the floor? Or was it simply giving the great man a big hand, which he needed somewhat, after being mauled and daubed a dove and an appeaser in the Cuba eyeball-to-eyeball aftermath? Undoubtedly I had goofed, but the Davis couple took it all very politely, and as they resumed dancing and fell back among the convivial crowd on the floor, the man suddenly brightened up and said laughingly over his wife's fair shoulders that I might probably be correct about the tail-end of my query.

From the upper middle-class club of AMSAC to the 'family' night gatherings that branches of the New York Public Library in Harlem sponsor in a sort of healthy rivalry among themselves, it is not really a long walk. These occasions, usually ones of friendly encounter, sometimes between local writers and their readers, and at other times on a triangular level with visiting African authors brought in, provide a 'culture' dose for those of the lower income brackets herded in Harlem as junkets downtown cater for the dilettanti whose one distinction, to quote Frazier, is an indisputable capacity for conspicuous consumption. Apart from that, the taste and indeed the fare are the same between both circles. Each asked me over as a speaking guest, and on each 'at home' host and guest were happy to part, never to cultivate each other's company again. Such was the unpleasantness and nausea felt on both sides, a professional hostess, who floats promotion parties for upcoming artists of all kinds, called for her smelling salts, took a sniff or two as my grandmother would her snuff, and turning to an equally embarrassed friend at one of these affairs, said in everybody's hearing: 'Of course, the young man may be a genius. But how can I possibly ask friends over to meet him when he shows such a penchant for making enemies?'

There was so much that was wrong with the house of the blacks in America, even among themselves and on the level of artists, that the most well-mannered cousin calling from abroad could not help but be openly critical – unless of course a primitive pride in the family and an equally primitive urge to clean it out and make the place better for all were lacking. It was a unique and rich experience sharing with the black citizens of America their growing excitement and sense of discovery towards Africa, a place only vaguely remembered by them before, and that with absolute shame and horror, from memories of an irrevocable fall, as Christians years ago recalled the doings in the Garden of Eden. Now, not only has this place they had been taught all their lives to look upon as a jungle full of fatal fruits and serpents turned out to be a rich and open plantation farmed all along by foreign squatters for their own benefit, but the black sons of the soil have at last actually risen and driven the exploiters back

across the seas from where they came. And it was no mean
or distant performances that could be kept out or distorted
for the ears of the people. Today, even the bum on Harlem's
125th Street, although he may not be able to read the *New
York Times* that prints all the news that is fit to print, and
although he may not own a TV set to tune to community-
minded stations, can see with his own eyes all the black
diplomats at the UN.

Going from one independent country in Africa to another
still burning to have its turn, I had observed a similar sense
of vicarious satisfaction and feeling of elation that the enemy
is at least out of the city gates, although other than those one
is defending. In the United States, however, the joy appears
even more intense among the emergent Negro. Their goal,
though is not the African one of expelling the host, but
that of kitchenmen, laundry-hands, motor-boys and noncoms,
all of them long restricted to the lowest ranks in the armed
forces for no just and legitimate cause, demanding at long
last a fair share in the victory and spoils with colleagues
really having no special abilities and merits to set them up
and apart in permanent positions of privilege.

Out of this new emotional response to Africa among the
Negro in America has come a great love for everything
African. It is all very heart-warming that a Negro can now
get up today and declare the roots of his origin even if he
cannot be as definite or far-reaching as President Kennedy
disclosing his Irish ancestry to Newark voters also of that
extraction. But when he goes collecting masks, and imitations
at that, without knowing their religious and social symbols
and observance; when he goes sporting drums, called over
there tom-toms, in blissful belief that anybody can beat on
them, however different in kind and intention, and produce
the famous talk for all to grin at; if he goes collecting music
from Africa and proclaiming each piece 'simple' and 'folksy';
then such an 'Afro-American', making a profession of his
faith among the uninitiated, more silly than cynical, must be

called to order before he misleads himself and others into total perdition.

A greater danger still is the habit of identifying this phoney, gushing business partly or wholly with the genuine historical stand of Negritude as established by Aimé Césaire and Leopold Senghor, or with the African Personality, to use Kwame Nkrumah's flamboyant slogan, which is better known in the States. There is an interesting feed-back here. The idea of the African Personality, especially in its political context, derived of course from the Pan-African Movement of Marcus Garvey and Dr Du Bois, and although both prophets naturally were never ones to listen to each other, it was to the lost black people of America they preached their sermons of Africa that must be redeemed, of an exodus back there, and of the glory and splendour that were its past. It is an irony of fate that today the black educated of America should be falling back upon the very doctrine they rejected and pooh-poohed half a century or so back. That they helped to hurl stones at both wisemen and still would deride them today should the two appear in Alabama or New York City may seem overstating the point. But both men are hardly ever remembered except by a few doubtful faithfuls squabbling on the fringe of Harlem's murky streets and slums. And more still, the spirit of union which has consecrated for better for worse several heroes and leaders in Africa, providing for each of their people a pivotal point, has apparently either by-passed America or presented her with so many candidates that they confound themselves.

On the other hand, what seems to dominate the field on the cultural front is the tendency among writers, editors and critics, college professors within the cult not excluded, to form themselves into associations for mutual promotion and admiration. As a pure reaction against a society that either from sheer indifference or discrimination strains from its main stream of literature works by Negro authors, this, like Negritude, would be a welcome stand and declaration, to create fresh new pools and channels out to sea. Unfortunately the current does not seem to be clear or cutting deep. Rather members of the club, swimmers, trainers and spectators alike, apparently prefer playing their own brand of game which is not bad, except that poor performances and low standards are everywhere applauded to the sky for the simple reason that they are by fellow members of the camp. And to thicken the cheers are the voices of patrons and promoters who naturally must be listened to and respected. Since everybody knows the rules, the patrons and promoters, usually honorary members from outside, play back the game by every time repeating the same fatuous and harmless platitudes and stereotypes like: 'negro writers express deep feelings,' 'the characters they create carry great humour and human warmth,' and 'the Negro hero is a simple, sweet soul.' All of this may be true but not the speciality or preserve of the Negro writer and people. And this is typical of the rich larding these people apply on their skin, a possible attempt to heighten or hide its existence.

Club members seeking compensations for a complex that shows them poor flounderers in life's stream of conflicting identities and links sometimes ask new-found associates from Africa whether there are any excavations for ancient and lost civilizations going on there, and if so, whether bards have sung them in epics. Not satisfied with the totem in hand, they would have broken pillars and parchments to convince denigrators like Senator Ellender that their black folks and cousins back in Africa did own and create something! At a Langston Hughes party in Harlem, I even heard the further claim that the first American cowboy, not just in literature but in real life and history, was a Negro. Like jazz and other great contributions of the Negro people to American culture, the whites had promptly seized upon it and stolen the patent. A most reassuring claim that was, especially as it came from Professor Rosey Poole, a white woman promoter of the association.

Under such pull and push, it is a miracle writers of real worth have emerged at all among the Negroes. The lately over-lionized James Baldwin, the long silent Ralph Ellison, and self-effacing Sam Allen who really is the poet Paul Vessey, and Papa Langston Hughes himself, everywhere styled the poet-laureate of the Negro people and the Shakespeare of Harlem, easily come to mind. But even these are often loved for the wrong works and for reasons merely sociological and extra-literary and artistic. Poetry, they say, should get as near as possible to music, but when music is made to replace poetry, then it is another matter entirely. Thus it is very painful to hear critics, otherwise perfectly sound and intelligent, picking on the 'blues' of Langston Hughes as examples of his best work when there is evidently a corpus of good poetry to the man. But such pieces are as much chosen for the 'authentic manner' in which they reproduce the 'idiom and rhythm' of the blues as for the virtue they make of being black, and black to the palms and bottom.

Undoubtedly, the temptation of the one theme and motif to choose and of what apparatus and form to present it in overwhelms many a writer, but more so should he happen to be black, and therefore of Africa or America. The tendency I found much more among black authors in America than in Africa, where it is menace enough, is to fall for the blackness of it and forget all art. In Africa both publishers and public unabashedly give a strong impression of praying for this to happen, but then it is a gimmick to be expected, as a great majority of them are at present European, and therefore still have to get out of that terrible hangover feeling of being in a special relationship with exotic and simple natives. Little wonder a lot of people today are making capital out of the theme of encounter, that is, of black meeting white, and the conflict and complication therefrom for the African. All this is fine timber. But it still requires a good carpenter and cabinet maker to turn it into beautiful furniture. Unless one is a gifted and genuine craftsman, what comes to pass for a work of art is a wobbly, ugly stool that should better have remained the piece of log it was before the author began hacking it around. And such logs do in fact make extraordinary seating in the square and market place in front of the ancestral hall.

Coming to the States, where indigenous publishing and a literate, local reading public should really be no problem, the black-white theme takes on fresh colorations, albeit of a leprous kind! The point, often so belaboured from the defending end here, is not that Negro authors write only about the Negro. Who else can any author write for and about except his own people he knows so well? The real quarrel is that most Negro writers see their subject at one point and position only – that of protest and prayer. As a result and perhaps without any intention of so doing, they have helped to create and establish a fresh set of stereotype figures and faces capable of expressing only certain simple emotions and gestures, none of which has to do with anything complex or cerebral, or with the mystery and permanence of the mask.

On the contrary, like the one-piece orchestra whose sole member is a piano, so much effort and energy has gone into pounding out of it the desired harmony, that spectators, especially if they pay to get admitted to the concert as is usually the practice, may well be forgiven and indeed praised for honesty and integrity if they hiss and grow restless on their seats at false notes and an undistinguished, in fact, appalling performance. A cry of 'Take to the cornet!' from somewhere in the audience would then be a brotherly act, not the taunting of a perverse critic. But that exactly was the angry reaction at a Harlem meeting to a suggestion of mine that for a picture of the Negro as a problem in his country it would be a far more rewarding exercise and experience to depend on a trained social scientist who documents the case with living facts rather than on some novelist palming off an ill-dressed and undigested story out of which sticks the contended bone of colour. An artist if anything should be an inventor, a creator of new things with use and beauty out of ordinary familiar pieces and material lying around. If he is content merely to rehash or dress up old stocks and frames better left alone or which anybody can perfectly well ham up if they have a mind to, then all distinction falls down, and we are again among the tinkerers and salesmen.

Rejection, however and not in the arts alone, is rotten eggs and tomatoes to a group protesting genuine identity, and demanding respect and recognition that ought to have been theirs by right of birth as human beings and citizens of the United States. Such natural acceptance and respect should not be a payment or bonus awarded to a few acquiring the right accent and desk. And when it has been so for as long as grandmother can remember, bottles and bricks should be expected in return – which is the healthy, virile, development now breaking out all over the American field and front.

But to borrow an image from James Baldwin, which he in turn was probably not echoing from the old spiritual but unconsciously from the Prophet Elijah's address to the first Black Moslem convention in Washington, the great fire to follow from bitterness, if not now directed and kept in control, will certainly carry disaster for all. For who is it to be turned upon? Upon the whites, of course, who bought the black-man and have kept him ever since in one form of chain or another in the land of the free. But what of the blackman's brother in Africa who sold him into slavery for a few tinsels and drink? And the Negro himself who all these years has been content to rattle his shackles, to breed behind the bars of discrimination, and to regard the debilitating cobwebs of so-called toleration drifting in Northern cities and states as the earnest of the covenant long promised in the skies. Joseph the Dreamer rose out of bondage to greatness and embraced his brothers who sold him into slavery, and they say, even forgave his foreign master Potiphar and the mistress who sought the damnation of his soul. Hearing Malcolm X, the Black Moslem torch-bearer, the Reverend Martin Luther

King, Junior, who had just been bombed out of his home, and Dr Roy Wilkins of the NAACP all address the first ever united front Negro meeting at Harlem's 125th Street, it was to me as clear as the rain that was pouring then that the leaders spoke in different tongues. Which of them was understood by the huge section of the audience that defied the path of thunder and lightning to hear the case for action, it is still too presumptuous to tell.

4 · AMONG ACTORS

'Here in Princeton we deal only with the classics,' Professor Downer of the English Department told me. 'But did you say you have written a play? And is it in English, if I may ask?'

I said yes, and the Professor was kind enough to offer:

'Let's see your play some time then, shall we?'

'I'll see if I have a copy left,' I said.

'Oh, it's been published, has it?' the Professor sat back in his chair and took a closer look at me. 'Was that in London? And at what theatre there did it appear?'

I told him I had not got that far yet, that I was completely home-spun. What there was of my career in the theatre seemed likely to snuff out there.

'Oh, no.' The Professor would not have me give up so early. 'If as you say you have written a play in verse that has been performed in several places in your native Africa, I guess you must have your hand on something. Now,' he added expansively, 'is this play of yours a comedy or tragedy?'

'I don't quite know,' I laughed nervously.

'Well, it isn't a one-acter, or does it run to three?'

'You wait,' I laughed more, getting up to go, 'and you'll see for yourself!'

The Professor rose up too, and as he saw me to the door, said kindly: 'Sorry we can't be of more help to you, but let's see your play sometime.'

From the McCosh where this interview had taken place I returned to the manager of my Princeton career at his offices in the Woodrow Wilson School building on George Washington Street. A huge, gnarled oak tree directly outside was being sawed down at the base and because the rattling of the motor engine made everything around tremble so, my manager's secretary and I had a difficult time of it hearing each other speak in the first room she occupied, providing a protective front and cover for the old colonel inside. But we knew each other well, and I went past her with the two of us giggling at the purring sound outside, and with hands to our ears. The Colonel too had his attention distracted to the doomed tree outside.

'You know they are moving this building some distance from here to make way for the new Woodrow Wilson –'

'Yes, I have heard the story that it is going to be moved bodily out of here. Is that true?'

'Well, it sounds crazy, but it's true.' The Colonel laid aside my doubts, sorting out in the process the several pens and pencils lying in line on his large table.

'It's hard to believe,' I said half shouting, half laughing above the throbbing motor outside.

'Well, so it is,' the Colonel conceded. 'But the group taking on the job claim they have moved a twenty-storey building down a whole block in New York, and not a single brick or glass pane was lost in that operation.'

'How do they do it?' I asked, honestly thrilled.

'Apparently, they first carve out and level up the ground round whatever structure they want to move,' the Colonel explained to me, gathering together again the pens and pencils he had been sorting out. 'Then they saw through the entire building at that basement level and drive through it appropriate rails and wheels. It is with these they slide the building out to whatever new site has been picked on. In this case, they have some two hundred yards to travel And as you can see, they need all the room they can get.'

'When is D-Day?' I asked. 'I must see the operation, whatever happens.'

'You are not alone there. All of Princeton, town and gown, is waiting anxiously for the big day. It should be sometime in the spring, although nobody knows for certain. But now, tell me,' the Colonel ordered the conversation to another course, 'how did you get on with the Professor?'

I told him the little there was to the story, and he was full of understanding.

'Shall I put you on direct to the McCarter people then?' he offered.

I said yes, and he promptly picked up his telephone: 'Is that Mrs McAneny? This is Bob Van de Velde . . . not bad . . . And how are you? Haven't seen all of you for a long time . . . I myself have been down with a heavy cold . . . Yes, Barbara has been running the show as usual . . . Well, I have an interesting young man here from Nigeria, one of our Parvin Fellows this year . . . Yes, he's a journalist in his country, but apparently has some interest in the theatre . . . Yes, he says he has written a play himself which has been mounted in his native country . . . That's good . . . Should I send him to you direct . . . Oh, yes, he speaks English . . . O.K. Then, over to you.'

I thanked the Colonel for all his troubles, and he said, Oh no, that I was welcome to all of them, especially as I had constituted myself into a one-man mission for my country, now asking for this and next minute for that other thing, all in the name of fair exchange and mutual knowledge of each other. He even walked half way to the door with me, and seeing me look at the doomed tree then just tottering outside his window, he joined me in the joke and hope that the ugly trunk would seek better vengeance elsewhere than fall over

the great Woodrow Wilson School building, which incidentally was itself being moved anyway.

At the McCarter Theatre, its General Manager, Mrs
Herbert McAneny, a stoutish elderly matron very warm and
bustling, accepted me instantly and on equal terms. Their
autumn series, which they captioned 'The Mediterranean
Heritage' was due to open that week or so, and would I
like to see the boys at work on the sets for Sophocles'
Antigone which was going to be the curtain raiser for the
season, as she showed me around? Yes, I said, I would
very much.

'Come with me then to the stage.' She took my hand, and
deposited me among the stage-hands. But they were all
clinging to and hammering away at the bleak backdrop of
the oncoming Greek family feud, and as one of them was kind
enough to explain to me several days after, I know very well
how at that stage of a production it is absolutely impossible
to turn the mind on anything else in the world, least of all
receiving strange visitors. All the same we became fast firm
friends, and there and then Mrs McAneny, in the thick hail
of tickets issued me two complimentary ones, the second for
my date, she was careful to explain.

'Well, I haven't got myself one yet,' I laughed awkwardly.

'Time you did, then,' she teased.

Later, she was to ask me to many more shows, and so for
me a fresh breath of air blew into the stifling house I had
come to find Princeton.

Somewhat of an artificial hand fitted on to the college, the
McCarter Theatre is not quite a natural organic part of the
body proper of Princeton, as Yale's School of Drama is with
that University. As a result, it has not much power of free
movement, and actually has not been able in its rather long
career to pick up new habits and exercises by way of experi-
ment as would a true living theatre. Instead, as is so aptly
put by Professor Downer who by virtue of teaching drama in
the English Department heads the theatre's faculty committee,

the McCarter Theatre busies itself only with the classics preferably as they appear each academic year on the English syllabus at Princeton.

'They are a trust body with their own resident company and quite independent of college control,' the Colonel had earlier made me understand. 'The one thing we expect is that by the time a young man passes out of Princeton, he should have had a fair chance of knowing his dramatic heritage. That's what the McCarter exists for, to present decent, respectable drama parents would take their children to at home.'

And true as steel, the McCarter in the season I was there rolled out a thoroughly proved and tested repertoire. Only like all things well tested and proved, this had been already safely done elsewhere by experts other than the present users. It fell in two parts. The first was 'The Mediterranean Heritage' we glimpsed earlier in passing, and it offered Sophocles' *Antigone* with the 'satyr' of *A Phoenix Too Frequent* by Fry on the same bill just as it was done in ancient times. This double, self-counter-pointing piece was then followed by Shakespeare's *A Comedy of Errors*, Albert Camus' *Caligula* and *Desire Under the Elms* by America's own giant of the theatre, Eugene O'Neill, all in that order. The other half of the season, running into the spring term, was straddled by the tall series 'Ladders of Ambition', with each terrible rung of it showing man in his various, vain fortunes. Thus it began very appropriately with *Julius Caeser* who as every school-boy knows was terribly ambitious and therefore had to die, brought in Moliere's *Le Bourgeois Gentilhomme* for plenty of belly-laughs more, it seems to me, at the expense of the Moslem and oriental Caliph than of the foolish French burgher, after which came in quick contrast Brecht's *Galileo* (to which the students' newspaper had urged everybody to take along their beautiful dates despite the ugly fact that the author was a dammed communist) and finally *Fuente Ovejuma* of the Spanish master Lope de Vega.

The last play, it was painstakingly pointed out in the programme sheet, was 'not really a proletarian manifesto' as modern left-wing producers would wrongly have people believe, but 'like all Spanish "golden age" plays and like much Elizabethan drama, it is primarily concerned with order and disorder; social disorder seen as cosmic disorder, and the restoration of order constituting a re-establishment of cosmic harmony under love.'

Of the entire McCarter achievement I recall two incidents, both perhaps slight in themselves, but because one provided for me a commentary on the calibre of the company and the management as the other did on the quality of the community and audience the theatre serves, they become quite significant. After *Antigone*, I stopped with Mrs McAneny at the box-office.

'Did you like it?' she asked me.

'Oh, yes,' I said, 'But why such an outlandish outfit for the chorus of courtiers or citizens at Creon's court? There was hardly any difference shown between them and Tiresias.'

'Well, you ask him!' she introduced me to a gentleman who turned out to be the executive producer of the place.

'You know it was a barbarous time,' he said wisely.

'Not so barbarous that they didn't live such terrific actions and emotions that nobody can beat them today.'

'Maybe that's true.'

'At least you could have dressed up your chorus a bit more differently. As it is, they looked to me like John the Baptist wild in the wilderness. That role probably coincides well with the blind seer's. And I'm sure you could have gained something by having women in the chorus.'

The gentleman kept his eyes down and his hands behind his back through all my harangue. Then he said curtly:

'We haven't got much money in this Theatre and therefore cannot play around too much with costumes.'

Later Mrs McAneny took me by the hand and to a party at backstage. It was a tame dribbling affair and under a pale,

running light people and furniture there took on eerie
shadows. But we caught one substantial person there all
right.

'This is Mr Stephen Porter, our guest director from New
York.' Mrs McAneny brought us together and left almost
at once. The director, a small neat figure of a man with a
sombrero hair atop him, expressed real surprise at hearing
the dramatic group of which I was a member while in college
at home had not only done the *Antigone* that Princeton's
professional troupe was now just tackling, but that we had
also offered a double bill of contrast in times and attitudes by
following up Sophocles with the Frenchman Jean Anouilh on
the same night.

'How exciting!' the director poured out some more cider
for us two.

I said yes, it really had been most exciting.

'But tell me, how did you manage it? Anouilh's *Antigone*
as you very well know is a full-length play, almost some
three hours, like any on Broadway. Now how did you
combine it with Sophocles? You must have had an extra-
ordinarily long night of it.'

'Not really,' I demurred. 'Some four hours running from
eight till about midnight, but people hardly noticed. We had
a tremendous Antigone.'

'What did you think of our own girl?'

'Well, I always thought Antigone a firebrand suddenly
flaring up and consuming in her flames herself and all those
dear around her.'

'That's correct,' he agreed.

'But your Antigone tonight, although showing the timber
necessary for her part, proved a rather wet affair, don't you
think?'

'Well,' the director began, then decided to leave the
matter at that point. Which was where we also broke up.

The other mirror scene at the McCarter was when the Le
Treteau de Paris, under the auspices of the French Govern-

ment which had then also loaned Mona Lisa to the American people for the temporary upliftment of their minds, stopped for a night at Princeton in their tour of the United States. They performed in their original tongue *L'Apollon de Bellac* by Jean Giraudoux and Jean Cocteau's *Orphée*. All the same, McCarter was filled to over-flowing that night in spite of this language dam. I was there myself, although without one word of French. But that was hardly the point. Hadn't I seen the fabulous Foo Hsing Theatre from Formosa (or the Republic of China as that country must be titled if you are not to stir up quills on the bad-tempered porcupine that is official America)? Yes, I said to myself, hadn't I seen that youthful troupe perform in Washington although all the Chinese I knew did not go beyond service in a Chinese restaurant? And hadn't I, like others enjoyed the gorgeous sets, the intricate dance and whirling acrobatics, even though their ging-gong, shrill, piping music had been a trifle upsetting, and hadn't the story of the loyal girl who offered herself as the beautiful bait that restores her king to his throne unfolded in superb action and mime? In short, I was well mounted on the high hobby horse that rides the theatre into a field of innumerable courses of delight, and of these language is regarded as simply one, not the only all-important source of pleasure. Here however occurred my great mistake. At the McCarter Theatre that night speech became the be-all and end-all of everything. Every single line, indeed every single word, called forth universal laughter in the hall. So much so that at several points, the players, obviously not used to this new kind of audience response, looked more than just pleasantly surprised and a trifle bemused and interrupted in their act. So bent was everybody there on impressing neighbours that they knew their French as it is spoken in Paris.

'Well,' I huffed in my seat, half in pique that I was out of it and half in real anger: 'Did Cocteau and Giraudoux ever get laughs like this among their own people?'

'The plays are really very funny.' My Dahomean colleague who came with me that night tried to calm me down. He was a real lady's man, and naturally felt great concern that several feminine crowns were at that moment snapping and tossing my way.

'Nonsense,' I snorted 'they are all terribly bourgeois here, and just showing off to one another. The plays, I bet you, mean little to a great many of them here.'

'Ssh,' my friend from Dahomey admonished me.

I obeyed, and almost from that instant, the rest was silence between me and the McCarter set-up.

As with my newspaper pilgrimage, after initiation rites at the local level, I made a profitable stop on my way to the central shrine of the performing arts in New York City. In fact, at that point both hosts led at the same time to Washington, DC, where they all but tripped up each other. I was there visiting for the first time as guest of the *Washington Post*, and Colonel Van de Velde, an old hand at planning out campaigns, had every move of mine arranged in such a way that it was easy for me to switch siege from the bastion of fearless, free writing to that of fearless, free speaking called the Arena Stage.

I had, when a child and at home, taken part in festivals and performances at the town square or market-place. While at school and college I had been taught classes on the theatre-in-the-round which they said Shakespeare's Globe Theatre, 'this round "O",' probably was. And of course since coming over to the US, friends and official guides and guardians had spoken of the open Shakespeare and college festivals I had to see in the summer to believe in concept of the round. But all this, it turned out, was not preparation enough.

The proscenium or picture-frame stage had in fact become the one image of the theatre fixed in my mind. So that when I came upon the Arena Stage in the city's Southwest Development area off the Potomac, I felt like one who had been fol-

lowing the course of a river and, just when he is thinking it is
one long journey with no turning, suddenly he is enveloped
in a whirlpool drawing over him all the force and flow of the
stream. The sheer architectural actuality of the Arena alone
was overwhelming. And so was its typical American career
of a Cinderella literally rising from rags to riches. Run by
the husband and wife team of Thomas and Zelda Fichandler,
the theatre is really a dream come true. To quote Brooks
Atkinson in *The New York Times*, it opened some thirteen
years ago 'in a decaying movie house that incidentally
supported a large population of rats.' From there, after
playing to 247 human beings in bleachers, the Stage, 'to get
off a treadmill that led nowhere,' moved in 1956 to the
'hospitality hall' of a dismantled brewery in the Foggy
Bottom area of the capital. By putting on a series of plays
that appealed to cultivated people – not forgetting casual
theatre-goers – Arena Stage made an impression on the life
of Washington, which has the second highest percentage of
college graduates of any American city, and the largest
assembly of psychiatrists – always a sign of cultural eminence
in a community. In five years the list of season subscribers
grew from 2,300 to 6,400.

For the Old Vat, as the theatre was known then, this
proved the turning-point in its whirligig career. 'Having been
a lively, cheerful, impromptu band of players and administra-
tors, not very seriously responsible to private stockholders,
it had to re-organise itself into a public non-profit institution
and solicit funds for a permanent theatre.' And this had to
be quick if it was to get out of the jaws of death then wide
open in the form of a new bridge over the Potomac. Fortunately, friends and foundations, and even tardy tight-fisted
merchants came to the rescue. They bought up bonds, made
generous grants, and gave gifts, if rather reluctantly, to
meet the grand total ransome of $850,000, the one portion of
the entire project that Brooks Atkinson rightly ruled is not
admirable. All of that to place a pavilion roof over a fair!

But Charles Laughton, visiting the Arena for the first time had cried 'Marvellous!', Sir Lawrence Olivier had exclaimed 'Fascinating!' and Warren Caro of New York's Theater Guild had called it 'the most theater-like theater', – all of which lyrical cries are closely recorded in the pages of the *Gentlemen's Quarterly* with President Kennedy on the cover. Mr Fichandler took me through the twin structure of the theatre, one rectangular, the other octagonal, and I was full of respect for the taste of its hosts and band of distinguished admirers.

The best photo-description of the stage when it opened in 1961 was probably that appearing in the London *Times*. 'The theatre,' it read, 'seats 750 in four steep tiers of eight rows, with an aisle running round the upper level, and overlooking that, a sequence of 11 private boxes. The south tier can be entirely removed for mounting plays in three-sided arena-staging rather than in-the-round. The stage itself, built in removable sections over an eight-foot well for special scenic effects (which includes access to electricity and even running water), is 30 by 36 feet, and a major distraction familiar to all in-the-round audiences – that of seeing feet and knees of the first row opposite caught in the stage-lights – is avoided by having the first row raised nine inches above stage-level and slightly set back behind a low, unobstrusive rail. Stage exits lead off at the four corners into a spacious passage, big enough both for the circulation of actors and the storing of scenery, running right round the theatre beneath the slope of the auditorium seating.' Very appropriately, Dylan Thomas's *Under Milk Wood* was showing at the time of my visit. The Fichandlers kindly asked me over in the evening and from a seat right in the front I saw the Arena company make a brave attempt to recreate Dylan Thomas's fantasia of a dreaming Welsh fishing port. Only the accent, not quite sorted out, was slightly disturbing to the ears, for which after all that over-luxuriant piece was written.

Washington, DC, which has more than her fair share of

flatulence from diplomatic cocktails and entertainments obviously is starved of a full offering of the performing arts when placed beside New York. But if one is a parish with the Arena Stage playing the humble devoted priest for whose services and support members of the community and flock make willing response and contribution, the other is one vast see without a bishop, or rather there are so many adventurers and claimants to the spiritual direction of an area, too large in any case for its inhabitants to share a genuine feeling of fellowship, that what should be an open praying ground has become a rigged market-place with services as commodity for sale to the sharpest bidder.

On Broadway which of course provides the heart of the mart, now almost all musical comedy, this is highly processed stuff, the better if wholly packaged and made to order, for then immediate, smooth distribution is guaranteed the production through the world-wide network of chain-stores owned by speculators and syndicates lurking behind assumed cassocks and frocks. And off-Broadway naturally is where a few fearless starry-eyed zealots and hermits have pitched their tattered tents and small stalls in a desperate if in-dividualist stand to halt a total fall-off in the number of faithfuls, and to win converts and customers to what each of them considers the original uncorrupted ware. I walked the hustling, suffocating rows of both sectors, gaining admission by various gates and on different credit cards, whether fake or genuine was difficult to tell.

Now, the common passage for a play on Broadway, if as is only natural it fails to show the sure patent of an Arthur Miller or a Tennessee Williams, goes something like this. First of course it has to be engendered and manufactured by the unknown hack of a playwright who submits it to the literary agent or broker in whose trays the new copy seeking outlet sits patiently with hundreds of others awaiting inspection. This may be for a week, a month, or even a year, depending on whether or not the poor unknown playwright

is an importunate hawker of his ware, and will not let the
telephone or the receptionist in the anteroom rest and so
forget him in his hunger and anger. The script eventually
gets read, after which one of three possible fates is spelt out
to its author: an outright yes or no (which is more often the
case); or the third, which is an offer proposing special points
of improvements and alteration the script must undergo if it
is to be presented further down the assembly line. This is the
critical moment for many a playright: to starve or to sell at
the new bargain price.

As the situation really allows for little struggle, the new
terms are soon agreed to between the inventor and the
broker, who in the name of dressing up the ware better for
marketing may jazz it up whichever way he judges fit. The
next step is highly professional, between the broker and the
merchant who will put the piece out on sale and arrange for
fool-proof distribution. 'Hell!' the merchant swears aloud
should he think he is being taken for a ride. Or he may
give the other a hearty slap on the back with a mighty
shout of 'swell!' if he fancies the goods and wants to buy
immediately.

This means money, at least $150,000 down on Broadway
to clinch the deal, an inflationary factor affecting even the
humblest out of the way production which must now be
above $20,000 to have a chance. Naturally, neither is a small
sum of money to be had for the asking by any merchant,
except of course if he has riches enough to enjoy credit rights
with the banks. So what does he do? He founds a liability
company, puts out shares for sales to members of the public
(which really is not all that public!). Those who buy up
shares are not so common and vulgar as to be seen in person
on the open stock market. They belong to special circles in
and out of the city, and any approach to them must be proper
and correct, preferably through the rounds of cocktails and
rare treats as among those of the smart and jet sets. Once
these are won over to backing the project, they become angels,

that nebulous band of promoters that literally supply all the force behind every scene on Broadway.

Sometimes there may even be oversubscribing so that you get that amazing and unforgivable phenomenon observed with the musical *Mr President*. For that show so many millions of tickets had been sold well in advance that the billboards proudly declared this was two years' straight delight guaranteed for all happy New Yorkers. But the piece, when it eventually opened after so much fan-fare and official promptings, was anything but the treat promised. And way out on the great West Coast, Ray Duncan reporting in *Playbill Magazine*, had this to say:

'Before the first curtain rose the Los Angeles Civic Light Opera had about $3,200,000 in advance season tickets sales in its possession, underwriting the longest and most ambitious season in its history . . . No other theatrical production group in the world,' he added a trifle superfluously, 'enjoys an advance sale of that magnitude.'

Thus even by that stage of the negotiations the programmes may just as well be written, for in the matter of actors and directors, who admittedly are the very life and blood of a production, any merchant-producer worth his salt will know just who and just when to hire and to fire. Usually, the stunt is first to interest some star who will play the lead, and there are not many artists living today who can resist the offer of a heavy purse, more so if the prospects for a steady income zoom in and out of sight like the firefly at night. And once it is well-known what bright name tops the bill, the other members of the cast are there for the asking – which is natural in a market already overcrowded, and where human stock runs so low that actors eke out a living by serving as waiters, ushers and cashiers in restaurants.

With all resources, financial and human, at last combined in their right proportion and mixture, the show moves out from the dark, labyrinthine reaches of the warehouse and factory into the shop, or playhouse, to use the technical term.

The respectable investors now retire completely out of sight to speculate on the outcome, recounting and crowing over past successes. The merchant-producer, since he is already on another deal, having satisfied himself that the bill-boards clearly stipulate that he is part or sole owner of the shop, also takes a discreet retreat and leaves the stage to the manager and staff that must now fashion out how best to offer the general public the ware they have sold themselves to sell.

One other tricky part of the business is that the shop usually is owned by persons other than those stocking it with goods. And because such persons have no preference for one type of goods to another, they let their shops solely for profit, and therefore quality with them holds no premium. As long as they draw forty per cent of the gross takings, the ware and its sellers and managers may as well go hang indefinitely. And how is the balance distributed? After running costs and staff salaries and taxes have been met, the playwright, lucky fellow, gets his ten or so per cent out of which the broker or agent takes his own ten or so per cent and the net sum becomes the preserve of the producer-merchant who will then make proper settlement with those angels fluttering all along on the wings of dividends.

I did more than just simply window-shop on and off Broadway, the world's largest shouting, I mean shopping centre for any kind of live or ghost entertainment. In the process I all but got sold myself into the bargain. Fortunately, there were about me always friends and officials who were most true and fit. Even before my arrival in the US, my friend Dick of Madison Avenue had written to say that he had on his own initiative sent copies of my play *Song of a Goat* to Mr Langston Hughes, the idea being that the old man who had contacts on Broadway would arrange a production with me on the spot. As it happened, I ran into Langston Hughes himself in East Africa in the course of a writers' conference called by Nigerians' art centre, Mbari,

at Kampala in June 1962. He told me that it was a real shame
he had up till then not seen a single copy of that play. Perhaps
his secretary had. I reported this to Dick in my reply to his
letter and there it might have all ended, since communications
sort of broke down between us two, had I not at the last
minute, so to speak, jumped the last plane for New York.
And naturally in our reunion the issue re-opened itself. But
it soon became clear to me that all my friend expected of my
play was a 'black' production.

'Why, Africa is right in the fore-front now,' he said in his
sincere winning way, 'and right here in the US the Negro is
in the consciousness of everybody. An African play by a
Negro group should therefore make an instant hit.'

'That appears to me pure politics,' I said.

'Perhaps that's so, but the show will sure be a success.'

'And the impression would be that a play written by an
African cannot be performed by white people,' I insisted.
'We act Shakespeare at home.'

'Oh, not that,' Dick objected, and I said petulantly, 'Oh,
yes of course,' after which we agreed to drop the
matter for the time being. It was never again opened with
anything like enthusiasm by any of us, and now that I look
back I regret that I rejected Dick's offer of help. I still do
not subscribe to the unabashed politics and publicity gimmick
he proposed for my play. But after seeing the lot of the
Negro, which in the so-called emancipated world of the arts
is even less a happy one and about which I shall have more
to reveal later, I regard it now a great loss of opportunity for
work and fun to many. Incidentally, Dick and I never
quite hit it off together again after this. Of course a couple of
telephone calls and letters passed between us, and one day
Dick even took me to lunch at the Waldorf Astoria. But there
were never more any serious talks or thoughts of a production, nor of the meeting he spoke of arranging for me with
friends and colleagues of his on *The New York Times* and
other top places.

Through Langston, with whom I became fast friends, more characters enter the story. Quite early in Nigeria and Uganda he had advised strongly against my accepting Princeton's offer of a fellowship for one whole academic year. Far better for an artist from Africa would be a few weeks' visit to the US, possibly on a State Department ticket such as I said was then in the offing for me. All the same, I had taken the Princeton offer and on my arrival there, dropped the old man a note since it was impossible to reach him by telephone. He had been away on some tour to the Mid-West or somewhere but wrote immediately he returned home to Harlem, although funnily not before the AMSAC people had fallen quite out of the blue to say the Poet Laureate of the Negro had told them of my arrival in the US from Africa, and could I please come over to New York sometime about Christmas and speak to the American people on the state of writing in Africa.

There was more to Langston's letter than words of welcome; it also carried an invitation asking me to the première of a new gospel play of his due then to open at some Jerusalem or Abyssinia Negro Church in Brooklyn. And so to New York city I went, losing several hours in a real Dantesque wandering underground that must have taken me to either Staten or Coney Island. Eventually, however I did arrive at the church in Brooklyn, a building that ironically used to be a playhouse. If the play, a loose-limbed affair stringing together gospel songs, spirituals, sermons and straight narrative about the life of Jesus Christ, had any merit to it at all, the production and performance that night hardly did anything to bring it out. Instead there was a running battle (with leaders and members of the choir all on one side and on the other the huge barrel of a pipe organ) as to which could pound and bawl best. The din over in the vast and almost empty auditorium, I filed out with others in obvious relief, and what was more, ran into Langston himself.

'Hi, John Pepper!' he gripped my hand.

'Hi, Langston!' I returned his warm clasp.

'Glad you could come to my play. But meet me in the foyer, will you? I must see some people right now.'

There was an exhibition running in the foyer. On display and obviously without discrimination were works by all sorts of Negro authors. I had not thumbed through more than half a dozen when Langston ambled back with a number of friends and admirers in full tow. I immediately recognised a large, black lady among them as the director and narrator in Langston's hit gospel musical *Black Nativity* which I had seen some weeks back in London. 'Vinette Carroll' Langston introduced her, 'And Barbara Griner' he turned to the pretty white girl with her. There were several more new names and fresh faces dropped at that point, and to all of them Langston presented me as Africa's greatest playwright!

'Well, let's go in somewhere and have a drink,' he said, and we trouped after him into the wan-lit night and cutting chill outside. No room in the first pub, but right next door some very understanding early customers moved over so that we could all four of us sit at one table. It was a tight squeezing job, but the beer came in quick and before long we were deep in it and in close cultivation of one another.

'So you saw our show in London?' Vinette laughed in her unique baritone voice, 'Barbara here co-produced it, you know.'

'I see – yes, I saw it on my way here and found it terrific. But why aren't you there now?'

'Vinette has been back home for some time now,' Barbara offered, 'but the show is still in Europe.'

'Do you know they actually drew the West End audience into spontaneous singing and clapping? It was so amazing a thing to happen with a people famous for their self-consciousness and respect that you could almost forgive those West End straight-necks for being out of step and tune,' I recalled.

'Oh, I miss London,' Vinette said simply, and for a few seconds we all sipped at our glasses of beer in silence.

'Any plans to tour Africa?' I asked.

'Oh, yes, as soon as we can raise the money. But the group is returning home first to play at the Lincoln Center in the Christmas week,' Barbara showed her cards.

'You must come to it,' Langston asked me, bringing us more bottles from the counter. 'You should see his *Song of a Goat*,' he told the girls.

'Oh, and what's that?' they both laughed at the same time.

'That's his play, of course,' Langston laughed back – 'the greatest in Africa.'

'Oh, you must let us see it so we can do it,' Barbara offered.

'Yes, you must send us copies; we'd love to direct it,' Vinette joined in.

'Of course he will,' Langston approved.

'I don't know if you'll like it,' I said a little confused.

'Oh, isn't he being shy now?' both girls laughed together.

Later with Langston gone one way, they gave me a lift in Barbara's compact car all the way to my lodgings down Washington Square in Greenwich Village. By now it was late and getting really frosty; so we exchanged addresses and telephone numbers, promising to meet again soon.

That was the last time I saw Barbara. Vinette I met again at Langston's during a small house party for the South African actor and author Bloke Modisane, then on a speaking tour of Negro Colleges in the South. Copies of my play did not reach me early either from my publishers at home or from Northwestern University Press, my US publishers. But as soon as they came in the New Year I called Barbara a couple of times while in New York. She was either away at her theatre, the house-keeper or maid would say whenever I rang the house, or when I called the theatre, some receptionist or secretary would say Mistress was away at the house. On the one occasion however when I got on to Barbara herself, she was too busy to see me, and her voice sounded so distant that I ran short of courage and didn't dare

go and see her on the Tuesday she said I should come over to
her theatre on 43rd Street by Times Square.

With Vinette, there occurred a slight variation to the theme
of alienation and drifting apart. She persuaded me to post
her my play for her to read in the peace of her apartment.
This I did, adding two others, *The Masquerade* and *The Raft*,
both of which I had just done at Princeton. For weeks
afterwards, I could not get anything out of Vinette. She was
either too caught up with teaching classes and with a play of
Archibald MacLeish she was doing or she was too baffled with
the several tax papers she had to complete for the revenue
people. I said that was all right since I was off to Canada
anyway to observe the April Elections there.

'Oh, I should be ready for you then,' she sent rich heavy
ripples down the line between us, 'and we certainly will do
something together.'

However, I returned from Canada in a fortnight, and
Vinette apparently had not moved one step or shifted from
her original position. The Macleish production still left her
prostrate and the income tax papers were still flying about
her as furiously as ever before. Now she was even thinking
of a teacher-director job in Africa. Wouldn't that be a fine
break, she asked. I said, of course, yes. And how was the
situation in Nigeria? Quite promising, I said, and that as a
matter of fact an old teacher and friend of mine had just
finished a recruitment drive in the US for experts for his new
school of drama at my old college. How sad she didn't know
about all this! Yes, I agreed, but then, I added, how was one
to know a famous figure like her would want to move from a
high pedestal at home. Oh that! she said. A break would be
great all the same. And is it possible to do anything now, say,
like getting in touch with this director fellow? I said there
would not be any harm in trying. And so on this low key
Vinette and I had our dying fall together in the matter of
reading and mounting a play of mine on or off Broadway.

A performance of another kind, also still-born, was the

proposal from the executive directors of the Columbia Lecture Bureau that I do a lecture tour of America for them. Theirs came as a complete surprise call one afternoon in December. As I was out on the first occasion, they left urgent word that I call collect in New York from Princeton. Next I had a personal interview with them in their towers close by Little Carnegie Hall. I was made to cool my heels in the anteroom by some secretary girl, after which I was ushered into the presence of a kindly looking old lady with pale blue eyes. Another more spare and sprightly came in through another door, and stood over me all through our meeting. They had launched a poet like Auden and would like to do the same with me from August to April! Would it be cheaper for all of us for me to return home first in summer as I had planned and then fly me back again for the tour, they asked. Or could I stay on in the US and be doing something in the interval? Anyway, all that could be settled later. And meanwhile I could appear on some guest programme of the Columbia Broadcasting System with which they had sister connections.

'Now have you a party card?' The kind old woman fired me a surprise query.

'What do you mean?' I laughed nervously.

'I mean do you carry a Communist Party card?' she asked pointedly. Again I laughed nervously.

'No, we are serious,' the other standing over me impressed upon me. 'We should like to know whether or not the Communist Party operates in Nigeria and if so whether you belong to them.'

'You need entertain no fear there,' I assured them through my laugh. 'The US still gives us aid.'

Eventually, however, we agreed that I mail them my work which they said Miss Frost, Robert Frost's own daughter and as much a poet in her own right as she was their own star reader, would advise them on the presentation.

'Have you, like the English, a title like poet-laureate?'

The kindly old lady fondled her hands. 'We'd love very much to present you as Africa's Poet-Laureate!' At that I laughed again and nervously too, adding to her obvious disillusionment that luckily for the arts in Nigeria, they were managing very well without the afflatus of some government-paid clown and lackey. After mailing my stuff to the august corporation sometime about Christmas and the New Year, I never heard from its directors again. At first, I thought the long illness and then the ripe fall of Robert Frost had prevented his daughter and housekeeper and bednurse, all combined in one, from acting in respect of an unknown African poet. But the months rolled by, and the sudden season of my departure came, and nothing happened, to quote the Wilfred Owen dirge.

Ruth Stone proved a different kind of companion and guide altogether. She and her husband Sam, a top engineer at the American Telephone Company, for whom he has recently co-designed the first machine to harness successfully the revolutionary principle of Laser beam, had come to my AMSAC talk just before Christmas with the simple aim of collecting more material for the thesis she was doing on theatre in Africa. Instead I became a rare piece in her collection! A couple of days after our first meeting, a long distance call was put on to me at the Graduate College in Princeton. It was Ruth calling. She wanted to produce and co-direct with some Nigerian Professor at Adelphi College my play *Song of a Goat*. Did I mind? I said not at all, except that my publisher's agent had just written to say Brandeis University had placed order for twenty or so copies of the play which must mean they wanted to do something with it. In addition, a Mr Martin Magner and his photographer wife, both of whom I had met at a Christmas party at Langston Hughes', had expressed a keen wish to have the play on in their own theatre at Youngstown, Ohio. None of this however would put off Ruth; as I soon came to know, she was impossible to resist. She was not in any sense a professional, she hastened to assure me, but for seven years had been the sole director of an arts centre serving the two million odd suburban community of Long Island. And it was for this centre so much like Ibadan's own Mbari of which she was a long distance member that she would like to co-direct *Song of a Goat* while I was still available for a personal appearance at the production. This she put sometime in the spring. Another proposition, more ambitious by far, would be a try at an off-Broadway showing with a mixed cast, but one or two people with name and money had first to be drawn into the cause. All this called for time and planning, and could I allow her a chance? That same week I took the train to Great Neck, had a big late lunch cooked for me by Ruth, and from that day on formed a firm friendship with her and Sam and their two teenage daughters Julie and Joanne that survived all my US strain.

The Stones took me to several shows in the city. Our first outing together was to the Metropolitan Opera for a performance of *Ariadne auf Naxos*. The night turned out to be rather remarkable. First, Karl Böhm, who had been a personal friend and colleague of the composer, conducted entirely from sweet memory with Leonie Rysanek in the lead, and secondly the opera, opened in English only to modulate violently into the original German. It left one somewhat rattled. But more interesting for us three was the seating plight in which we found ourselves. Perched on a couple of decks high on the steep cliff that is the side of the huge ugly stone quarry they call the Metropolitan, we could only see the players far away and way down below us, who looked like pin-headed puppets tripping up in a pirouette. The fall of the curtain after the long prologue and induction came therefore as a real relief.

'Come with me,' Ruth called to Sam and me. Her restless inquiring eyes in and out of her spy-glass had spotted a box by the stage right at the other sheer fall of the hall. Only one lady sat there in solitary glory.

'She won't let us in,' Sam protested.

'Oh, why not? She's all alone and surely wouldn't mind our joining her,' Ruth swept us along. Next she got hold of a distinguished looking usher, and before the old man knew what was afoot, prevailed upon him to lead the way to the box. 'Can you resist her?' the old man threw wide his hands when I could not contain a laugh. So into the box we all marched.

'Here you are, lady,' the usher bowed us in.

'Yes, thank you so much,' replied Ruth, bowing out the man. And then turning that same winning smile of hers upon the lady seated inside, she stated simply as a matter of course that we had come to swell her company.

'Well, that's all right by me,' said the lady seated inside the box, 'except that the box is not mine really.'

'Oh, that's fine, then,' Ruth soothed her, and looked over to Sam and me to see how comfortable we were in the seats she had already settled us in. Then the curtain rose for the opera proper, and with that fell our joint fortunes. A solid shadow of a man emerged suddenly, darkening the entrance to our box.

'Please come back with me to your seats,' he said briefly and with supreme blandness.

'Why, the lady here invited us in,' Ruth remonstrated with him.

'Sorry, madam, but you don't want me to lose my job. So come with me, please,' the shadow said in a voice still more portentous than fate.

'Oh, surely the lady who owns the box does not mind our staying,' Ruth insisted, appealing to that august personage. But no help came from that high state. Instead she said:

'Oh, no, I told you the box was not mine,' and then she added something to the effect that she was the wife of some manager or director at the Metropolitan, but by this time we had been marched out and consequently lost her mumbling in the music then pouring all over the place. On the way, Ruth, irrepressible as ever, steered Sam and me into another private box, this time occupied by its legitimate owners, an elderly couple who regarded us sternly in turn through their lognettes and then very wisely returned their attention to the business on hand. We had not even bothered to say hello but flopped straight into the first empty seats we saw vacant in the box.

We went to several more shows together, Harold Pinter's two plays *The Dumbwaiter* and *The Collection*, in a double bill off Broadway, and John Gielgud's star-studded revival of *The School for Scandal* supplying both ends of the beat. I arrived for the latter in heavy snow and on a train more than two hours behind schedule but got in all the same ahead of Ruth and Sam. They found me on the outskirts of a large crowd crushing their way through the foyer of The Majestic.

'There must be lots of celebrities here tonight,' Ruth drank the scene in at one go. 'Have you spotted any?'

'I wouldn't know them,' I said in my innocence, and a woman with a face pock-marked with frost and glowing like boiled prawn snorted in distaste. The show itself, though of the highest polish possible, well proved that old proverb saying all that glitters is not gold, for shallow behind the shine of the nickel that is the play lay its incontrovertible core of rust and mould.

Even worse and more of a worthless experience was the matinée of *Chin-Chin* I attended with Ruth. The Plymouth Theatre was filled to overflowing chiefly with matrons, their girls at home from colleges, and younger sons still at preparatory schools. Such was the irresistible draw of Anthony Quinn and Margaret Leighton, the stars of the show. But theirs were properties of gold washed with sediment down the drain. The protagonists were an unhappy couple jilted severally by their original partners; Quinn had no real trouble portraying the dark, warm, Italianate construction-engineer and husband seeking solace and consolation in the arms of the abused English wife he meets in a posh New York hotel, but Miss Leighton, a real sybil if ever there was one, and worthy of the stage and screen, cut a terribly, poor, pathetic figure as she tried stripping to her skin and bones to awaken manly passion in her new found partner. The only feelings she succeeded in arousing however both in her lover and herself were those of disgust and disillusion. And you could not have agreed more with them. But, on the contrary, everybody else there seemed to have had the greatest treat of their lives. The big names, the special promotions and press parties, and the thoroughly automatized props, now creating with a mere flick of lights the vast Pan American Airway building complex in a void, next spreading out with a click of buttons the entire parched sprawl of New York's lower East side, not counting the pale songs, speech and dance that provide the staple for musicals so standard now on Broadway, were all there as auto-suggesters and prompters to laughter and cheers.

'Coming behind stage to salute the stars?' Ruth asked at the final curtain call.

'Not for a thousand stripes!' I said in my most surly voice. Sitting as a stranger in stalls, show after show, and especially after watching Vivien Leigh, undoubtedly 'one of the crown jewels', dazzle her way through a *Tovarich* anything but bright, I came to find myself more and more foxed by a common riddle: which deserved the other, the public or the production?

The answer they told me lay outside the vast bazaar in the desert called Broadway. So one week in March I did a grand tour of the few independent stalls making a stout job of resisting the utterly commercial sway and character of Broadway. My first place of call was the American National Theatre and Academy, 'an organization of theatre services, information and activities, Congressionally Chartered' so its brochure proudly declares, 'and independently financed by its members and interested donors, dedicated . . . to extend the living theatre beyond its present limitations by bringing the best in the Theatre to every state in the Union.' I spent my time admiring ANTA's letters of commendation from the State Department while the young girl at the reception desk tried to check up whether I really had a previous appointment.

But Old Colonel Grumpy from his emporium at Princeton had
seen to all that so I was soon in the presence of handsome Mrs
Ruth Mayleas, Director of the National Theater Service
Department. She met me at the door with a close colleague
of hers, a most charming woman. Plagued by a terrible habit
of not paying attention to names when meeting new faces, I
did not for quite some time know which official and personage
exactly I had then the pleasure of meeting. So there I sat
between my two hostesses fidgety about which side to move
my chair nearer, and which warm smile I should return first.
Fortunately, two outside calls came in almost at once, and for
a brief gorgeous scene, it was quite a joy watching these two
women executives chatter away at the same time, each on her
line to a different caller on a separate subject. In due time I
came to know who was who.

'Now you know who we are,' Mrs Mayleas finished
briefing me. 'ANTA serves as a national theater for our
country, represents her abroad on international bodies like
UNESCO or ITI, and when theater people from other places
come over here to the US, it is our job to show them the right
things to see.' And that was what she would like to do with
me. 'Are you thinking of publishing some of your poetry
here?' she asked.

I said yes, that is, if it was not too much trouble. To which
she replied: 'Oh, no, magazines like *Evergreen Review* would
be pleased to hear from you. And what about a drama
magazine? *The Tulane* would be just right for you.' I took
all these down.

'But you must be wanting very much to visit the Actors'
Studio.' She changed the subject and picked up the telephone
at her desk.

It turned out that the great director of the Actors' Studio
Mr Lee Strasberg was away in Moscow for a Stanislavski
anniversary and festival. His secretary did not know exactly
when he would be returning. In that event classes at the studio
could not sit that Tuesday. But Thursday should be all right

for the visitor from Princeton, no, Africa, and everybody at the Studio would be delighted to meet him.

Before leaving, I gave Mrs Mayleas copies of my plays.

'I'm not promising we'll put them up at our theatre,' she said frankly.

'Oh, no,' I said, 'I wasn't expecting that. They are just for a keepsake.'

'Well, thank you very much,' she shook my hand. At this point, her associate and friend also rose, and with care almost maternal, both walked me to the door and out into the corridor beyond.

In the meantime Ruth had been waiting for me at another famous and even more individual stall a couple of streets and avenues off Broadway, where ANTA has itself installed by Times Square, and there I went through the slush of early spring and screaming stream of traffic to join her. Coming from Princeton with its Institute of Advanced Studies, first directed by Albert Einstein and now by Robert Oppenheimer (to whom I had a note of introduction from Melvin Lasky of *Encounter*, but got no reply), the name of the stall, that is, the Institute for Advanced Studies in the Theatre Arts, rang familiarly in my head. Ruth was something of a supporter and assistant to the founder and director Dr John D. Mitchell. A solid silent American Brahmin, I ran into him at the head of the staircase. After our brief introduction by Ruth, who never missed a chance of touting me, Dr Mitchell walked back with me into his office.

To answer my queries about his establishment, he gave me one or two brochures to study in my spare time, but meanwhile he suggested that it would be a great idea if Ruth took me to the studio and workshop theatre to watch his visiting German Director rehearse a specially selected cast in their current production, Bertolt Brecht's *Good Woman of Setzuan*.

'Yes, that's what we really want to do,' said Ruth. 'The drama group at his college in Nigeria actually staged the same play some time ago. Now he wants to compare.'

'That's fine,' Dr Mitchell approved and left us to ourselves.

Founded in 1958 by the doctor and his heiress wife Miriam, IASTA, as the institute is affectionately called by those of it, invites leading directors from different countries every year for six weeks each, to analyse and direct in English translation a theatre classic of their respective countries. Actors usually double as assistant directors and other staff are enrolled members of the institute, the aim being 'to increase the American theater artist's chances of studying at first-hand the styles and techniques of foreign theater traditions and to help meet the challenge of theater forms other than the naturalistic, true to life style in which he excels.'

I had the privilege of being asked to appear on a Brecht panel and was most disappointed at not being able to do so because of the gathering build-up at Princeton against my extra-mural activities. But I did make a closed-door discussion led by the German director. Also there that day was Mr Alan Schneider who a few years back had directed *The Caucasian Chalk Circle* for the Arena stage in Washington, DC, and had a current hit with Edward Albee's *Who's Afraid of Virginia Woolf?*, a family fracas among faculty members and wives too long by a half and with an end that might just as well never have come at all; it came out of nothing in the third act. Mr Schneider made it clear he always tried to do what the playwright wanted done, but one thing he was still not very sure of was all this talk about the East Berlin master's method. Didn't the master himself show a change later? And how many of his apostles and disciples now really agree among themselves? At this stage of the discussion, with the German thumping for words to get across through an official female interpreter with whom several other unofficial ones disagreed quite often, I ventured to mention that at Ibadan we had gone straight for the play and did not appear to have lost anything substantial to the theorists in the process.

'Oh, no, that wasn't what I meant at all,' Mr Schneider quickly put the record straight and poor me in my proper

place. Notwithstanding such differences and denials *The Good
Woman* that had looked so raggle-taggle at casting and rehearsals achieved realization late in March far much greater
than anybody had dared anticipate.

Apparently, the Actors' Studio is even more of a dealer in
rarer, original ware, or at least so it lays claim to be. Founded
by Elia Kazan, Robert Lewis and Cheryl Crawford, its aim
was that 'the development and stimulation of the individual
talent would create a trained ensemble of actors that could
serve as the necessary and essential foundation for a theater'
– which really is people. Just before I left the United States
in May, members of the club had for the first time in their
history, and indeed of the theatre anywhere, got themselves a
playhouse on Broadway all on their own initiative although of
course with generous gifts and funds from perennial benefactors like Ford. Yes, it is rare for ordinary members to steal
the lead from the boss, but members of the Actors' Studio
happen not to be simple ordinary folks. A look at the cast for
its first production, the slow pallid marathon of *Strange
Interlude* by that giant Eugene O'Neill, provides a representative picture of the stars within the studio's galleries. Betty
Field, Ben Gazzara, Pat Hingle, Geraldine Page, Geoffrey
Horne and others on that cast are names scintillating on the
American sky, over-crowded with constellations. On the day
of my first visit there new admissions included Sidney Poitier.
Nor has the Studio quite forgotten those exciting days, not
far gone, when Marilyn Monroe though not really a member
used to attend classes under the personal tutorship of Mrs
Lee Strasberg.

Snobbery seems therefore to be a danger to the real
wares of the Actors' Studio. Quite understandably, it scowls
at glossy catalogues and brochures for self-advertisement
and hands out instead only a few sober sheets of typewritten
matter to those who care so much for the state of the soul of
the theatre they seek what salvation the studio has found for
it. The Studio boasts of auditions topping the thousand mark

every single year, and out of all this only a bare average of six get the great privilege and honour of being selected. To my query whether this was symptomatic of the present rot in the theatre or merely the exiguousness of room I got a somewhat stony stare not completely void of a snub. What is more, members of the Studio must be working actors, directors and playwrights. In a market where there are many more wanting to sell than there are articles of value, this to say the least sounds a hard if not absurd test.

I knew a girl who was the proud winner of the national award for the best supporting performance of that year. Her quiet, delicate, and self-absorbed style came out clear even in the Studio under the baleful eyes and dog-eat-dog criticism of colleagues and incipient rivals. In that brief scene I saw her in she was an air hostess back in town, meeting in a bar after several years her first boyfriend, now a married man and father. He would like their affair to start again but she has already been through many ports and nothing is exciting to her any more. Playing opposite her that day was a popular TV star on New York national networks and the complaint from her as well as the young man who directed them was their difficulty in getting away from the personal magnet of the man. Several weeks after, I saw the same girl a second time, this time on TV and on somebody's show featuring Ella Fitzgerald and Duke Ellington. Her toothy grin was unmistakable, and so was her poise and self-assurance. In such circumstances who would have thought she had been out of a job for weeks past? But in her open uninhibited manner, a little loud perhaps, she laughed that she was fast getting used to queueing up for her weekly dole from the Social Security people. And what became of her membership card at the Studio while she was not working I do not know.

Still more niggling is the unemployment factor when applied to those of the American theatre who happen to be black. Obtaining a regular job on or off Broadway calls for patent assets and of course a certain amount of luck and the right connections. A black skin, however, is a sure liability, except of course in those proverbial caste-typed parts of slave or servants. Producers of Broadway, like the publicity men of Madison Avenue, are so full of respect and regard for the feelings of their white sponsors and clientele they prefer not to take the risk of ruffling and offending their tastes by using coloured people in roles where they are not normally seen in real life as lived in a vast area of the United States of America. Respectable citizens switch on their TV sets or buy tickets for a play to get relaxation and amusement, not to be reminded of the ugly and unpleasant facts in life. Indeed it may safely be said that all they pay to watch is escape stuff, fairy tales like *Oliver* with all of Dickens' teeth and talons extracted and taken out of it. The story even goes that so touchy has this issue become, a show was put on about the subway riders of New York without a single dark face showing! This was elimination and escape through the foulest pipe of all, for who else walks most the dark underground of New York but the sweltering oppressed blacks?

The politics of colour however seems to be permeating today the entire American scene, and changes for the better and more normal are therefore becoming actually visible to the naked eye which does not view things from coloured glasses or through inverted telescopes. And in the theatre world, when I was there, this was nowhere more evident than the appearance of a Negro judge, albeit silent, in an episode of the famous TV serial *Sam Benedict*. Perhaps the long run of Genet's *The Blacks* at St Marks', featuring an all black cast in a blistering assault on white supremacy before an intimate audience almost all white night after night is an indication too of the present civic rights upheaval now promising to change the face of the land. But until it is reasonably complete good actors, directors and playwrights, only incidentally of a different colour from the majority, will continue to find it doubly difficult getting a regular day's job. I had a girl friend who was in *The Blacks* but had been out of

it and of any other bill for more than a year. 'A theatre for
the Negro people!' she used to cry. And all her hopes of
getting one were centred on an organization like AMSAC
who in turn would solicit aid from white genii like Rockefeller
and Ford!

Another confusing point about the conflict between the
promoters of the straight unashamed commercials of
Broadway and the few champions for quality and talent like
the Actors Studio is the sliding one is likely to observe in the
scale of standards.

From the high pedestal of a panel discussion within the
precincts of the Actors' Studio, pundits like Lee Strasberg
himself and that great exhibitionist of emotions and director
Harold Clurman would declare in one breath a score on
Broadway nothing to go by and cite example after example of
success – all of them, it seems, from Broadway! There must
be method with a capital M, they insist, a marriage of mind
and action not just among the actors, director, and playwright,
but one between them and members of the audience, for it is
only after such a fusion the play finally arrives out of the
script or copy originally submitted. Yet eventually, it is the
box office takings that come to count!

One must not be too uncharitable and churlish. The task
facing the producer-director with a mission is no mean one.
It seems to me a change has first to be made with those he is
out to serve. The American spectator-public is touchy about
many things. It avoids colour like leprosy, and eschews
anything demanding thought or dealing with attitudes and
beliefs foreign to its conditioned consciousness. Thus a play
like Brecht's *Mother Courage* with Oscar-winner Anne
Bancroft for the principal part never had a chance of getting
to the public's heart. Contrary to the excuses that were given
about chronicles, caption drops and waits for scene-changing,
I rather incline to believe that it was the theme of play that
sent away the public in droves, leading to closure in under
three weeks. And the view over Broadway is littered with the

corpses of many a promising recruit, although it must be added by way of epitaph that a good number of them died prematurely as they deserved, uncommitted, mercenary, lifeless and unsung.

One such disaster, in fact, a double one involving Max Frisch, became also my misfortune. His *Andorra* was opening on Broadway and 'off' at the Maidstone was his *Firebugs*. Both were to open in the same week in what, despite the newspaper blackout, was rightly touted through notices on radio and TV as well as service calls on phones as a Frisch Festival in New York. And to be there himself the Swiss German dramatist flew in all the way from Europe where these same plays were already playing to crowded audiences in more than sixty playhouses. Naturally, I felt very close to the whole show, for wasn't Stanley, the producer of the second piece, also going to do my play with Ruth his friend? So one drivelling night Ruth, Sam and I drove over to Stanley's for what was intended as a launching party for a show that had been put off more than twice or so before. 'Where's Max Frisch?' I asked, not seeing anybody infested by all the other guests as houseflies crowd a cube of sugar. 'Away in Mexico,' Stanley laughed very manfully. 'He was so upset he broke his glasses and took off immediately with his pretty secretary to Mexico.' As the saying goes, we did not at that point know exactly whether to cry or laugh. But Stanley was laughing again and passing us more sweets between drinks and the dishes to come. *Andorra*, he said, had opened, was it Wednesday or Friday, and closed the same night. His own show (we saw it at rehearsals, didn't we?) opened on Thursday. 'Come over one day before it folds up on Sunday,' he laughed. 'Oh, sure, we will,' we said in one hollow voice. But Stanley knew as well as we did that there would be no such day and we all settled down to what for a funereal party did not lack the frenzy of mourners wanting to forget a loved and lost one. And with that also faded my hopes of a production on or off Broadway.

5 · THE AMERICAN DREAM

De Tocqueville's history is still held to be America's best testimonial. In the one hundred and thirty odd years since it was given, the great rambling loghouse of America all but fell down in a heap, as foreseen by the visiting Frenchman. True, old Abe Lincoln who was then head of the house gave his life in spite of himself to preserve a semblance of family unity. But bonds between the feuding relatives were already badly broken, and attempts to have them forged again have since proved a mockery. For not only have they resulted in the uprooted statues of the South being put up again and indeed on higher stands, but the so-called freed black bondsmen of the family lost their iron-cast chains only to be turned into ragged tramps and squatters on God's own rich estate, which they had sweated more than beasts of burden to build.

Almost at the same time and in the long harrowing aftermath of reconstruction and reaction, members of the small band of robber barons, operating on railway and shipping lines as well as in vast mines and banks spanning the entire continent, were piling up by hook or crook their fabulous billions on the ruin and rise again of the American house. In the predatory process, they established for the good of all that great American myth and apologia of the self-made man, the smart guy who makes good where all others have failed. Later came the universal crash on Wall Street after the Great War, and for a short but terrible period there grew the real scare that the entire structure and fabric of the house that the Yankee had built handsomely for himself would cave in and collapse. But that amazing cripple Franklin Delano Roosevelt was prompt on the scene, and what the colossus of Wall Street, J. P. Morgan himself had failed to prop up with his indefinite stock of dollars, the cripple successfully mended with words of comfort for America's forgotten man, holding out the promise of a New Deal for all. His firm, resourceful hand, especially during those first hundred days of his long rule that like Napoleon's last were so full of fate, may have effectively plucked the firebrand of revolution away from reach of hordes of arsonists then roaming the American estate. But it must be said that it took the outbreak of the Second World War that was the wreck of others to put limping America back on her feet, and flood her house with yet more ill-gotten gains.

All these are events and adventures enough to mark or change for ever for good or bad the face of any hero or idol. But quite on the contrary, the one image that America would like to see of herself has not only remained untouched and unbruised where all others have lost either limb, head or life itself, just as it is with those super imperishable heroes of wild west brawls, but its native owners have made it an article of faith to defy every visitor to dare deny that the American fetish and shrine is the one and only true, supreme and eternal cause to worship everywhere. Within a week of my arrival in Princeton in September 1962 it became clear to me as branches on trees stripped bare by autumn that the constant concern of every American I came in contact with, from the professor to the professional hostess and even the publican, was to convert me, an unbelieving foreigner and

African. Indeed the shock seemed to be that this was necessary at all; the gospel really ought to have reached and sunk into me already.

Princeton however was not taking any chances with us Parvin Fellows. There was a special seminar we had to attend every Thursday afternoon from just after lunch to before supper all the days of our stay there. It met regularly at a library in the Woodrow Wilson building, and always the subject for sale was American Civilization, as if knowledge of this was all we needed to make us better able to perform our various duties back in our own countries. We were not addressed immediately by that charming salesman of American ware Mr Max Lerner. That was to come later – in the winter term, and when discontent began to show visible if undeclared on many a face other than my perennially sullen one. The first session we ever had I remember like an afternoon dream. Starting out severally from our individual minor pursuits for the day, participants soon converged at the place of pilgrimage, and rather hushed and as if expecting some revelation any moment, we all took the one road and staircase to the library. Already waiting there at the head of five heavy tables in horse-shoe formation and behind a pile of books, sat Colonel Robert Van de Velde, one-time of the US Army and an acknowledged authority on psychological warfare. Sharing the place of honour with him was a slender taut gentleman of thirty-five or thereabouts: Professor Shaw Livermore of the History Department at Princeton, and a fellow member of the great Democratic Party of America on whose platform he was at that very moment seeking election as an Honourable Member of the Borough Council of Princeton, as the Colonel introduced him. The rest of us from abroad found our natural positions down on their either side.

All in all we made quite a collection, perhaps even more so than the old piece hung up there on the wall showing the august signatories to the Treaty of Versailles with Princeton's own President Woodrow Wilson in prominent display: a journalist from South Korea, another from Poland, an agriculturist from Haiti, a general (unfortunately not in uniform) from the Republic of Somalia, a diplomat from Syria, a literature licentiate of the University of Dakar from Dahomey, a junior civil servant in the Prisons Department from Nigeria, a lawyer and research fellow from Yugoslavia, and poor me known simply as a journalist from Nigeria and wanting to be accepted too as an artist. 'We miss our Indian friend who should have been with us here today,' the Colonel announced solemnly. 'But much as he wanted to come with the blessing of the Indian Government, he also happens to be directly in charge of government information, and right now is training all the guns at his command on the Red Chinese at the North-west Frontier.' The lesson had begun.

But first of all, there were recommended books to distribute. The reading list included *The First American Revolution*, a glowing account of the Thirteen Colonies on their Eve of Independence by Clinton Rossiter who in 1954 'was chosen by the Fund for the Republic to direct a scholarly survey of Communist influence in American life,' Edmund S. Morgan's *The Birth of the Republic: 1763–89*, a study, in the Chicago History of American Civilization, of the high ideals that raised petty protests over tax to a historic fight for freedom, and *The Nation Takes Shape: 1789–1837* by Marcus Cunliffe who tells, again in the Chicago series, of how dream and reality interplayed to form an undying democracy for America under Washington through to Jackson. Other authorised readings for the Parvin group were *The Response to Industrialism* by Samuel P. Hayes, yet another epic from the Chicago pantheon, Frederick Lewis Allen's *Only Yesterday*, greeted by the London *Spectator* as 'the most important book written about America,' A. A. Berle's over-smooth story *The 20th Century Capitalist Revolution*, and bringing up the rear in grand finale was *The New Age of Franklin Roosevelt* by

Dexter Perkins, fittingly again in the Chicago History of American Civilization.

'We had thought of issuing you these books to use for the duration of your programme here. That would have meant collecting them back from you just when you are thinking of returning home to your various countries and would want to take along with you real fine studies of America.' Colonel R. W. Van de Velde deployed the tools of persuasion piled in front of him. Then he went on, 'But we now think that the best idea would be to make you buy them, that is, at a token fee of $10 for the whole lot. Now that's a real bargain for you.' He managed a laugh down his triple chin, pushing out the books for us to pass for inspection among ourselves. Not that there was really room for choice; each title on the authorised catalogue had to be read for the weekly seminar that came to form a rigid if hollow heart to the course. 'Now, over to you, Professor,' the Colonel turned to his colleague. And for the next three hours and more we were taken by way of a map sprawled out on the wall on a full tour of the vast unknown wilderness across the seas that religious zealots and fanatics, first from England and then Europe, and other characters destitute and desperate for gold, land and freedom, all in that order, farmed in a matter of a few years into the nation that today is the mightiest, the richest, and the freest man has ever set eyes on since the sun rose first on the chaos that was then the universe.

The account we heard that afternoon and were to hear dinned into us in one form or another day after day was one not unworthy of the deed. But most remarkable perhaps was the double figure of the old Colonel and the young professor silhouetted as a piece against the ochre parchment on the wall, one with stick in hand, the other supplying a running commentary, as they led us headlong in the footsteps of America's intrepid pioneer and founder, first in his settlements stringing the Atlantic seaboard from Maine and Massachusetts to Virginia and Florida, then up through the

Mississippi and the Ohio and the Missouri behind the Appelechians into the Mid-West Plains and deserts, and finally over the Rockies through passes scaled only by help of military expeditions after the Civil War and the round-about passage of the Panama into the gold rush and sunshine of California sprawling unexploited between Canada and Mexico.

Even more significant, when the marathon exercise was over, as became still more evident with other sessions and professors, was the image of the Colonel sitting at the head of affairs, solid and silent like a lighthouse, but every now and again breaking in with a rare flash of illumination to offer correction to any inadvertent misstatement made by his learned colleague who may not have had at his disposal all the facts as officially interpreted. That one unchanging 'testimonial' by de Tocqueville had just faithfully to be adhered to. And true to test, the occasion always called for polar comparison. In the good old days it used simply to be 'America is all innocence and Europe all evil.' Today the formula, now a warcry, has become 'The US is God-fearing and free while the Soviet Union enchains, and is of Satan's party.' This kind of effort seemed to me rather like that of some middle-aged careerist in public life for ever seeking assurances from others about his success and achievement. It hardly matters that those he seeks to impress have little or no interest in the subject. But because he is not very sure himself that he has fulfilled all the promise and predictions his all-wise teacher set out in his school-leaving testimonial, he would very much like others, and they need not be his superiors or equals alone but any junior and subordinate as well to say to his hearing and comfort that he has not done a bad job of it at all, but in point of fact has positively made good.

Now, as everybody but the narcissistic Yankee well knows, Alexis de Tocqueville wrote his *Democracy In America* in 1831–2 rather more in hope and expectation of what America the overgrown, acquisitive youth could become, especially when compared with the thorough mess of a career Old Mother Europe had made for herself, than in praise or appreciation of anything then in actual practice anywhere. The Utopia and theory had not quite been achieved, even though the American founders seemed to have had all the fair chances of starting on a fresh slate. There were however, fine traits he saw developing in the child that had run away from home to be on his own, and these if fully developed should make of him something near that ideal figure towards the realization of which the older countries of the world seemed to have forfeited their chances. The Frenchman observed and analysed a number of these qualities and attitudes which he thought peculiar to the people he was visiting. Chief of them were the American's idea of commerce and trade, his concept of a classless society, his suspicion of a government strong and purposeful at the centre, and his belief in equal opportunity, that every citizen has a right to a fair and open share of what there is of the land and nature's bounty.

All these remain fine and high ideals, and nobody denies that the early American founders and pioneers, among the later breed of whom de Tocqueville moved during his visit, did in spite of their rapacious tendencies have a creed to live and fight by. Thus one of them, John Quincy Adams, could proudly say: 'Revolution took place in the minds of the people in the fifteen years before Lexington.'

An unshakeable belief in the personal ownership of property and the right to protect it with all the means possible as never enjoyed by his fathers and brothers back in Europe lay behind it all. 'I was drying my saddlebags,' says the gentleman in Pound's Cantos, 'and four yeomen in the bar room were talking politics: "If," says one, "they can take Mr Hancocks' wharf and Mr Rowe's wharf, they can take my house and your barn." So he was ready to take up gun at once not only in the unequal fight with the original owners of the land he was tilling by the labour of another, but also as soon as Congress cried out against tax prerogatives of an imperial master overseas.

And if things got too hot and uncomfortable in Boston with the whole town hunting him down as a witch or disciple of the devil, the old intrepid American tiller could always sell up his farm or brewery, hitch the family fortune to a waggon, and with the Bible and a true-barrelled gun in hand, set out further afield to carve a new place for himself in the sun and virgin country still unexplored and open to the claim and title-deed of first come first served. There was always the chance of moving out to try again one's luck and pluck if the initial strike and hope that brought in the first instance the settler out of oppressive Europe happened to prove vain. Today however, the frontier has vanished for ever from the reach of descendants of men and women who trudged miles into hostile forests and deserts leading nobody knew where. 'Oh, you exaggerate!' said the political professor. 'Surely an American still enjoys today a degree of mobility and choice obtainable nowhere else in the world.' Yes, if an American packs his job up in one state or city, the chances of a break for him in another may still show reasonably even. But that is not saying his trail will parallel that walked by his forebears. The very fact that he would be looking up to another for employment belies the comparison. The pioneer before him was his own master with God himself as confidante. The automobile may be a wonderful improvement upon the wagon, and the fact that one can always stop a few nights today in motels, however synthetic their hospitality, is a prospect less dangerous than walking into the righteous ambush of Red Indians. But arrival at last would be at a stereotyped industrial centre into whose inevitable whirl and pull the present-day adventurer soon gets sucked, and if he is not fast and firm with his grip, a clean sweep-out into the vast cess-pit of more than six million unemployed and bums may well be the wages, for all his independent striking out.

In the cold light of this vision of a horizon really already lost President Kennedy's slogan of New Frontiers opening out to Americans suddenly falls into proper perspective.

But it seems hardly likely the ordinary American citizen (in so far as any American is ordinary at all!) will want to shed his testimonial and dream. Just before Christmas, I took a cab in New York in order to be punctual for a talk I was scheduled to give that night. Like most cab-drivers in that city, mine turned out to be most talkative and forth-coming, and before I had plumped into my seat, we were right away on a quick exchange of the latest news. It was blackout time then with the newspapers. And as it so happened, on our route we drove past Times Building.

'Look over there!' The cab-driver pointed out the pickets about the place. 'They are workers on strike. Not even President Kennedy can tell them to go back to work. Now that's the great thing about us in America. In Ghana and Russia they'd all be shot.'

I laughed out loud which rubbed him up the wrong way.

'That's the honest truth,' he declared. 'The President can't ask me to go out to work if I don't have a mind to.'

'Yes,' I said as sweetly as I could, 'why should he – when it would be for the profit of some other person no freer than you? Over in Ghana and Russia you'd be working in state-owned plants. So why should you strike? You'd be killing the plant you pay yearly tax on.'

'That's right,' the cab-driver licked his lips. 'I never thought of that.'

Later when he dropped me and in my hurry I tipped him more than I should have, he leaned out of his car-window and almost whined: 'Brother, but I don't get this business of state owning plants.'

'How could you?' I called back, and ran straight into an elevator going up.

At Edison, a real industrial hub off New Brunswick, I had

been put on the carpet for the same reason by a group of big industrialists and businessmen gathered there for the opening of a new factory making new types of electric lamp shades that diffuse light evenly about a room. This was during my visit to *The Home News* in the course of which the paper's industrial and scientific reporter (or correspondent as he preferred to call himself) invited me out in his Herald Coupé, about which he was full of apologies, principally in respect of its small size.

'You come from Nigeria?' They all swamped me, making me look every big indeed.

'Yes,' I said, turning to as many of them as I could take in at once. 'And when are you going to market your wares there?'

'Not immediately,' said the managing director of the new plant. 'Our plans don't extend even to Europe yet.'

'Tell me,' some big shot cut in. 'Why do all you new African states go for state-ownership of business?'

'Oh, not really,' I said.

'Of course so,' another cut me short. 'I happen to know in Nigeria the railways, ports, power, mines, and even broadcasting are run by government. And isn't that the pattern all over Africa and Asia today?'

'Don't you think those industries you have mentioned are too vital to leave in private hands?'

'A real communist fellow,' someone muttered at the outskirt of the crowd about me.

'One thing you don't know –' I began.

'And what's that?' an impatient director snatched at my tongue.

'Well,' I said, 'those state industries you speak of were really opened by the British.'

'Oh the British!' Several there stamped their feet. 'Why couldn't they let the citizens themselves develop their own resources?'

'What of capital –'

'And of the know-how.'

'No, those fellows just love fouling up things so the communists can make a quick take-over.'

There was much more musing among those men of money assembled there that day to prospect for profits, none of which they were prepared to risk on the African market.

'I know your politicians are corrupt fellows,' one patted me on the back, 'but tell your President – you are a journalist, aren't you? – Well, tell him industry is safest and best in private hands. See us here in the US? That's what we have gone for all our lives, and today we'd do it all over again.'

I thought of the US Postal Services run by government and I could not agree less with the man. Letters are delivered only once a day and unlike Her Majesty's mail, that must go on, any local holiday is enough to hold up progress of the US Mail. At that moment too, two lines of Pound came into my mind –

> and the fleet that went out to Salamis
> was built by state loan to the builders

but I thought better of it and kept them to myself.

The old credo of the right to private property and of the inherent ability and right of man to exploit an existing opportunity for wealth sounds as good as ever in the American ear. It little matters that with the collapse of the frontier the chief articles in the creed have also lost all their foundations. The Vanderbilts and Stanfords have built for themselves and their heirs all the transcontinental railways for which Congress in Washington, DC, granted them sole rights as well as all resources above and beneath the ground ten miles on either side, thus spelling the ruin and rise of many a city and state in the Union. Similarly, and side by side, if in cutthroat competition, the Rockefellers and Andrew Carnegies have tapped all the vast wells and mines even though

thousands found in them their common grave. And so did the
J. P. Morgans unto their heirs for ever –

> Robbing the public for private
> individual's gain . . .

with their world-wide chain of discount banks binding government and individuals alike fast about their feet. In such
circumstances what equal opportunity to wealth and power is
there left for the present generation American to exploit in
the true spirit of his fathers when all the corporations,
accounting for a preponderant proportion of the nation's
resources, are long since safe and sound in the hands of a
few families and females estimated to be no more than a mere
six per cent of the entire people? But this again is a futile
query to throw at any American.

Once on a trip from Ford's Mahwah assembly complex,
the largest in the whole world, situated at where New York
State stands shoulder to shoulder with the State of New
Jersey, I recall asking the Colonel about the ownership of
America's giant corporations like General Motors. 'Why,
we Americans,' he said promptly, and with obvious pride
added for the peace of my mind: 'My wife and I own a
number of shares in General Motors. And so do thousands of
Americans.' Now to be fair to the old man, I remain quite
ignorant of how large his holdings are with the Chevrolet
people. But it is not unusual to meet a proud American
investor who because of the ten or so shares he has bought
on a huge corporation claims equal ownership of it with a
Ford and the true heirs of a Du Pont. So accommodating is
the heaven of property and free private enterprise, everybody within enjoys absolute happiness even though one
capacity may be no bigger than a jug's and another as large
as the Atlantic.

Against such a backdrop it becomes doubly fascinating
to overhear the debates now going on, in the hollow halls on

Capitol Hill, over new vistas of wealth like aeronautics and satellites communication. Who is to own them? Is an industry valued at billions of dollars and developed with taxpayers' money to be signed away by government to a private monopoly group? It had been done before, when General Ulysses Grant of Civil War fame granted perpetual concessions to the Robber Barons who exploited their mines and railways at public expense and with public bonds. And in this present day and age the same principle has been in full operation since and during the War, with the granting of sole manufacturing rights of nuclear and other heavy military equipment to a closed cartel. This is free private enterprise, indeed not unworthy of that saying by Christ that unto them that have more shall be given, and from them that have not even the little they have shall be taken away and added to them that multiply their talents abundantly.

It would be interesting to watch how the advocates of state-ownership fare further in the debate, especially now that one of their most outspoken men, Senator Estes Kefauver, has fallen, mortally wounded in action, so to speak. And if the Kennedy Administration, as in many other issues, refused to show its claws, it may well be on account of the simple fact that a strong central government is a red rag to the champion American bull who will charge and pull out all such administrative claws at any sign of their showing. That surely was the cause of racialist state Governors like Ross Barnett and Wallace, of Mississippi and Alabama. But Federal Troops moved in all the same as a worthy band of matadors, and probably the whole world outside South Africa was their aficionado! But resistance to government advance is certain and unbending on other fronts more vital to the American if less celebrated. I quite remember once an advertisement carried in a national newsmagazine. The message? Rally round the banner of private enterprise, it exhorted all true Americans. The Federal Government has made inroads into the power supply business other than with its damned Tennessee Valley project. If you don't take a stand now and dislodge all those socialist agents, you sure will lose the entire field!

Now, the fun in this hue and cry was that more than eighty per cent of the power supplied in the United States has always been in the control of private hands. It is also significant that it was in this very industry that some of the most notorious anti-trust prosecutions have been made in the United States. Top-ranking executives in the nation's largest electrical houses were probably at that time still serving sentence in Philadelphia for fixing equipment prices, sharing out the market among themselves, and keeping out all others from contract awards in a tight monopoly vice. As a result and part of this free enterprise frenzy and craze, the American housewife has had to pay for her electrical services (which goodness knows she needs in the factory of her kitchen) at a rate that has risen by more than sixty per cent since the War as against an increase in other consumer fields ten times less than that.

But as de Tocqueville well stated in his testimonial, America is one vast house of chance and contradiction, with a structure unwieldy beyond understanding. And truly as that French noble predicted, the house so divided deeply against itself was a few years after one vast hall of death. Of course the slaughter of brother by brother exhausted itself in five years, but the outcome proved so delirious that the victors abandoned the stand for the defeated who went further and dug themselves in deeper than before. Since then, although the terrible mess was all cleared up, ghosts have haunted its gilded halls and walks. And to this day, as family members from Massachusetts engage themselves in a running row with others from Mississippi over the natural rights guaranteed the individual, black or white, by the American Constitution, birthrights which the school song innocently proclaims are enjoyed from the city of New York to Birmingham, the visitor from abroad, not won over by the conducted tour and the lavish board, may well wonder how long this union of several disparate, self-repellent elements can last. But then many a marriage has survived on some rock of convenience undiscovered to the gossip columnist!

6 · THE AFFLUENT
AND FREE

I often had to remind myself that Americans come of emigrant peoples, drawn from all sectors of the compass under all kinds of circumstances, pioneer peoples who crashed every barrier to a continent closed to the world until Columbus stumbled upon it, founding fathers who debated the slightest domestic problem in the open town-hall of their settlements surrounded everywhere by wilderness, and who, possessed of no power beyond a mulish insistence upon abstract common rights given all mankind by God, successfully broke the initial yoke thrown upon any overseas peoples by the biggest imperial bully of them all. So ignorant and almost fascist, so stay-at-home like a wall-gecko, and so conformist and scared of any talk of change were most Americans I met or viewed in action and accounts, that I found it difficult connecting them with their original revolutionary stock.

My first shock was at the respectable hands of a Princeton businessman who asked me to lunch at the local Rotary Club. The lady in double-plated jacket behind the reception desk at Nassau Inn threw me a doubtful suspicious look, probably for showing my face in the premises at all, but immediately I said I was the guest of a gentleman whose name I gave her,

she sprang out round the counter-bar, switched on a smile
that showed me sweetly all the way to my host, who, she said,
was already inside the dining hall and waiting with his
honourable friends for the visitor from Africa. There I
joined them, a very distinguished gathering indeed, except
that so many princes and overseers of industry and business
were there present, each in his pavilion and stand, that it was
folly for a stranger visiting the fair to try telling one tent
from another. I accordingly contented myself with remaining
by my host, generous (as most Americans are), and a textile
magnate. But taking the floor that day was a most inventive
representative from the Johnson and Johnson complex, a
gentleman, at one time the sole staff of that federal agency
examining all new drugs before they make appearance in
stores all over the Union. And like the multi-inventor George
Washington Carver, for whom he had the greatest respect
and no colour label, he was seeking patents for several wares,
ranging from boots and tyre soles to surgical gut and possible
covers for sausages and hotdogs edible as well as durable.
And all of these came from one basic source and raw material,
namely, rubber.

'Better apply to be the new Johnson man in your country,'
the gentleman across the table laughed in my face.

'Not a bad idea,' I laughed back.

'Belong to the Rotary Club in your country?' my host
asked.

'Unfortunately, not,' I said 'for that's real class.'

'Oh yes,' everybody laughed. 'Really the best passport you
can get anywhere – from Afghanistan to Venezuela.' A
member who had just returned from India shifted in his seat.
'Actually brought in that flag up there only the other day.'
We all looked up at the flag-board on the wall.

'No, I guess your country isn't up among those yet,' my
host read my thoughts.

'By the way, what part of Africa is Nigeria?' he added.

'Oh, on the West Coast,' I offered.

'Now, Ghana is your capital city, isn't it?'

'No,' I said. 'Ghana and Nigeria are two separate states entirely.'

'No?' he fixed me with his fork. 'Now that really is news. And is Nigeria north of the other then? Excuse my asking, but these new countries in Africa, they are creations of the British and the French, aren't they?'

'Quite like the thirteen Colonies, aren't they?' I wanted to say, but then the gentleman from Johnson and Johnson was already up on his feet and fingering his notes all carefully laid out on the table, and to him we all turned our attention, and with great profit too it proved to be. Later, my host, still meaning no offence, ate up my sweet. 'Or did you want some?' he regarded me gently. I tried a stale joke. 'No, I feel sweet as I am!'

'Now, about Nigeria again, if I may ask,' he shook out his serviette and wiped his mouth in no great hurry, 'how large a place is it?'

'Now let me see,' I said, 'it must be about the size of Texas and Oregon put together.'

'What's that?' someone leaned over to hear better.

'He says Nigeria is as large as Texas and Oregon put together.'

The gentleman leaning over whistled softly to himself. 'It must be a very large city,' he said.

'Not a city but a whole country,' I said pushing back my chair. I was beginning to get tired and hot.

'And what is the population, do you know?' my host followed on.

'About one-fifth that of the US,' I said.

'Wow,' they all leaned forward together, nearly bumping their heads in the process, 'the place must be overcrowded!'

Such ignorance of the outside world or rather the total assumption by Americans that the word ends with the United States, with Europe perhaps as a mere historical extension, and the first of those old holes that the US for her own safety has to seal off from the red rats, provided for me a rude concrete barrier against which I bruised my shins again and again. And it was not confined to just the wealthy and white who could very well afford to live, thrive and die in their individual cocoons completely insulated from the rest of the world. I once took out a black girl in search of fun in New York City. Black, by the way, was just the one adjective to make her fingernails rear for some flesh to tear to pieces. Our first meeting had been at that AMSAC banquet for African Ambassadors to the United Nations. She was no black or Afro-anything but a Negro she had told me in no uncertain terms, and a Negro, she gave a clear definition, was a combination of the strains of all the peoples in the world. And when I asked whether any one of these strains could prove dominant, she replied that the combination made her a new distinct whole. 'How spirited you are! This is the first time I have had my own fire turned back on me,' I confessed to her.

'Is it so?' she smiled, and moved over to my table shawl and handbag. 'I might as well,' she added, 'my escort is no great shakes. See him there dancing with someone else? But you Africans are different. You sure can talk!'

'And act too!' I added, calling her a drink.

Marlene was an actress with great ambition and hopes, who had appeared last on *The Blacks* when that show opened in New York to offer white liberals and masochists and penitents the one therapeutic treatment they had long been after; but that was almost six months ago, and since then pretty, vivacious Marlene had been a good-humoured guest of her parents far out in Brooklyn as well as of the Social Security people. And there I turn up, a real playwright! Would I please write her a part? Of course, yes, I promised. As a matter of fact, she might well fit into the plans just then taking shape for a production.

And so in the meantime Marlene and I went out in search of excitement, a quest that landed us in the exotic lap of *The*

Village Gate in Greenwich Village. Cat, Israel and their friend Naomi with whom I became quite close made up the company. Music literally poured in from all sides that night, from the magnificent voice of the blues and folksong queen Odetta, for whom the microphone will always be superfluous, from the combo drums and brass of Herbie Mann, who had not forgotten the beat he picked up in Africa, and from the harmonica of the ingenious Adler who ranges from jazz to Bach. 'We must go out more,' Israel suggested, himself a good musician on the 'cello. 'Cat's father, you remember, is a first violinist in the New York Philharmonic. We all should go and hear them sometime.'

'Wouldn't that be great!' I agreed.

'Sorry we haven't taken you to see more of the city,' Cat joined in.

'Oh, I should love to see the Zoo.' I jumped at their offer. 'I missed it in London coming out.'

The sandwich Marlene was eating stopped half-way to her luscious wide mouth, and her eyes, unusually bright in the dim light, bore straight into me.

'What do you want to go to the Zoo for?' she asked in a sharp voice.

'Why to see the inmates there,' I explained. 'I'm dying to see those lions, elephants, tigers and all my other wild cousins in there.'

'You miss them?' Marlene looked real scared.

'Haven't seen any of them before in all my life,' I disclosed.

'No, are you kidding? Don't those creatures crawl your village like automobiles here?'

I gave her a light smack on the shoulder, accompanied with a loud yell and laugh.

'Now you are laughing at me!' she pouted in her spirited way. 'All my life I have been taught Africans live on tree-tops among those animals. How should I know you'd be coming to New York to see lions for the first time?' It took a couple more beers and sandwiches, Naomi and Cat joining in the latter, to wash out the sick taste now on every tongue.

The point was often made, and conceded sometimes by me, that America is actually a continent and not just an ordinary country. To know her in all her amplitude and fifty odd sprawling states must therefore require specialist interest and knowledge. Of course, lots of Americans I knew, and they were not necessarily privileged or belonging to the exclusive jet set, did quite some travelling in and out of the Union. Thus in the course of the holiday season lots of the New Yorkers would flock to places like Cape Cod or Miami and beyond. But for the majority it seems the Union centres around their individual states and cities, which is good patriotism, except that it is not uncommon to run into perfectly literate and sophisticated Americans, like one young lady friend of mine from New York, asking me at Princeton in New Jersey to look her up in the city on my way to Washington, DC, way down South at the other end as the plane flies. 'I come from California,' had been her excuse.

For a candidate, however, for ever seeking election as the champion of what the slogan calls the free world in opposition to the flaming red devil and dragon, such an excuse would be lame indeed and holding up no real shield. Even in ordinary local politics, the candidate has first to tour his constituency and make himself familiar with the faces and facts of life of those he aspires to represent and lead. Maybe this is asking too much. Today, any candidate can handshake, buss and bribe his way to the heart of the most remote and difficult electorate, and this is the path that Americans, being a practical people and government, have chosen to tread. One danger, however, with all straight and short roads is that they often are the death of the antelope.

'You hold back your votes and we hold back our help,' was more or less the frank and cordial message high executives at the USAID division told us Parvin Fellows during a session with the State Department in Washington. General Lucius Clay had then just issued his report to President Kennedy calling for a trimming of sails and a bailing of ballast out of a boat whose actual trouble was not any sea rougher than normal but a crew and perhaps captain who often showed nothing but awkwardness. 'We have all the funds, equipment and experts to supply any country soliciting our help, yes, even communist countries, but we demand not simply a native hand willing to plan and work as we direct but also a heart that will for ever say thank-you to the American people.' Later, at the various divisions serving the different member countries we held even more frank and cordial discussions with divisional heads. The man for West Africa had just returned from a working tour of his beat and had a lot of local news from Nigeria. 'Was that country getting her fair share of USAID?' I asked. 'I ask because the US has as yet no military bases there, and the bogey of a communist take-over does not stalk her as in other places. As a result, it seems that much smaller states, and not just those satisfying the twin prior conditions above, are getting more aid, although it is a pity, reports say, that this often is frittered away, less by corrupt local politicians than by US experts ill-loaded with privileges and tax exemptions, most of whom have little or no sympathetic touch with the people and plan they are despatched out to serve.' His Excellency listened to me patiently to the end and then in his soft purring voice, while his junior at his side sat spinning circles on his note-book, spoke confidingly of the just and fair principle of aid awards.

'Oh yes, Nigeria gets her fair share,' he assured me, and then with a twinkle in his eyes added: 'Even now moneys and men are ready any minute for release to Nigeria, but your governments still have not asked for them.'

'Is that part of the $80 million given a year ago before I left home?'

'That's right. With a federal set-up such as you have, it has not been very easy making allocations to the individual regions without appearing to favour one to the disadvantage of the others. But we are managing all right and we all expect great things of your country both on the continent of Africa and in the councils of the world as a whole.'

Americans, very true to their candidatural role, like being liked a lot by foreigners. The picture they cut is of a big shaggy dog charging up to the chance caller, in mixed feelings of welcome and defiance, and romping one moment up your front with its great weight, all in a plea to be fondled, and in the next breaking off the embrace to canter about you, head chasing after tail, and snout in the air, offering furious barks and bites. 'Where you from?' they breathe hot over the stranger to their shores. And before you have had time to reply, they are pumping and priming you more: 'How do you like the US? Do you plan to go back to that country? Don't you find it most free here? In Russia the individual is not free, you know, he cannot even worship God as he likes and make all the money he should.' And from this torrential downpour of self-praise the American never allows the overwhelmed visitor any cover, actually expecting in return more praise and a complete instant endorsement. God save the brash impolitic stranger who does not!

That in a small way was my fate at the loving hands of a Baptist church in Trenton, the capital city of the State of New Jersey. A chapter of ladies, not exactly the Daughters of the Revolution, anxious to welcome graduate students from countries abroad, communist countries not included, asked those of us at Princeton to come over one Sunday afternoon for tea. The cards, or invites as they call them over there, were all conspicuously signed by a certain Miss Harriet who made it very clear that the girls were all most willing and anxious to make friends. So all of us who were invited, bachelors as well as grass widowers, trouped over to Trenton that Sunday in cars made available and driven by several kind ladies. I rode in a Cadillac, a mother's loving gift to her daughter when she married more than ten years ago, and all this for me was a real pleasant surprise, the only one of the day, as it turned out.

First, it was not a tea party after all but a tepid punch affair,
served liberally from bowls by two august women who with
noses all crinkled up showed no obvious relish for the fare
they were filling others with. Next, our dear Miss Harriet,
the exact physical opposite of her namesake in Guy de
Maupassant, had passed the age of discretion and had been
safely beyond all desires a long, long time ago. At that
moment, she was actually bowing her way out of the scene
she had for years dominated. The third and final shock I
personally could not bear and rose up against was a roll-call
of guests, already invested with badges telling their names
and countries of origin, and the request, it was more like a
command, that each stand up before the full church hall,
announce to all there his name and nation, and recount for the
gratification of his hosts how much he liked the United States
of America. Which apparently everybody there did very
much. Only a few, to the silent moral disapproval of all
present, pleaded neutrality on grounds of their short stay
so far in the United States. But, foolhardy fellow that I was,
I threw all discretion and courtesy to the winds, and gave the
great romping American dog a rather vicious kick on the
backside, sending a terrible hush down and up the whole
house.

Later, one or two sour-faced inmates sidled up to me:
'This is freedom of speech as it can only be enjoyed in the
United States,' they drooled. And one middle-aged woman,
something of a squatter in the place and sporting an Italian
accent, stole a quick glance this way and that, and then
hurried over to me to offer her surprised cheers: 'Only you
Africans from abroad can afford to tell them the plain truth.
We can't here, you know, having settled here for so long.
But do you know, our children – my first boy is in the Army
right now doing his national service and the girl after him is
at college – they are all on the bandwagon, you know, and
sometimes their father – he works in a garage – he and I kind
of wonder if our children are not even louder at it than most.'

Having unburdened her bosom, she looked this way and that
a second time, and scurried off, leaving me more exposed
than ever, for nobody at that stage of development would be
seen near me.

Nor was this the only punishment for my outrageous
behaviour. Some weeks after, a letter came in the post for me
from Trenton. I could not recall anybody there except the
laundry people. Nor was I anywhere the wiser for opening
that letter. It bore no address, no signature. All the kind
correspondent had to say was this:

'Dear Mr Clark,
    Please bathe more frequently.'

Shadows of anger and amusement raced across my face in
quick vivid succession. A mathematician from Chicago
sharing the same entry with me calculated something was the
matter, and on reading the letter, suggested I see the
Princeton people or the pastor of the Baptist flock. But I
thought better of it, particularly of the latter, having no
mind at that time of day to get immersed in ablution matters,
bath-wise or baptismal.

Brain-picking was another habit of mind for which I could
not stand many Americans. One April day in particular
there had been so much picking that I felt emptied and
pinched all over. First came a long distance call from the
Nigerian Consulate-General in New York. A certain
professor at Columbia wanted to start classes in Modern
African Literature, and very much wished to have me over
in the city for lunch that day. He wouldn't take no for an
answer. As they had put him off a lot of times before, they
could not help but accept his invitation without first consulting
me. Would I please accept and not let the home side down?

I told them yes, provided they would talk the matter over
with the Colonel himself who alone could excuse me from
attending the great Parvin seminar due for that afternoon,

since the man was already full of frowns for my many outings to address groups as different from one another as college students and faculty members at Cornell and Adelphi, Unitarian church women at Princeton, and diplomats bound for Africa from the State Department in Washington DC. They called me back a few minutes after to say they had successfully carried this off, adding for my benefit that the old Colonel had said I was a very bright talented young man but one obviously needing to see more of the United States to understand and admire its people, and that task they were still trying to perform with me! The eleven-thirty Suburban Transit bus took me into town in under two hours. An old university colleague was on hand to collect me; so we drove straight to the Columbia University area where we eventually located our professor host inside a Chinese restaurant. Tired of waiting, he said he had cancelled his booking and finished a quiet luncheon with a guest from the Ivory Coast who kept time. Anyway, could we start on our discussion of new African authors? This was the signal for his systematic plying of me with questions about the vision, the point of view, the philosophy and so on and so forth of Nigerian writers, especially the novelists, from Tutuola through Ekwensi and Nzekwu to Achebe. And every word I said he gave me the impression of cataloguing away for future use and reference. Later, at his apartment uptown, when he had eventually found the right key out of a huge bunch to let us in, we had some argument about these authors.

'Well, you have them here in your library, haven't you?' I asked rather heatedly.

'Of course, yes,' he took my challenge. Promptly he found his way to an extensive rack against the wall but he could not fetch the volumes we wanted even though one or two of them were staring us right in the face. The fellow didn't even know his texts, and he wanted to teach others African Literature! I got furious in my own short-sightedness. A week afterwards I heard that my professor friend had gone stone-blind. He had first fallen ill aboard an aeroplane somewhere over the Atlantic, and that short day of our meeting had been the tail end of a twilight fast failing into complete darkness. And I had taunted him for trying to be smart with me. I felt rotten for days afterwards.

With others, however, that day and elsewhere, I still have no sympathy. I returned to Princeton that April day to find that some publishers wanted me over immediately to their place for supper. Co-guest with me that night was a very learned man, Dr William Spaudling, sometimes something of a titular head for the publishing industry all over the Union. After a rocking handshake with me, he resumed the folksong he was singing with the young married daughter of the house, whom I thought I had seen before singing folksongs of all lands to her own guitar accompaniment at the Princeton YMCA some time during the Christmas season. This was his last night home before flying to Europe and Africa, Nigeria being one of his stops. In fact, host Dr Datus Smith, the Director of Franklin Publications, and guest had only recently returned from a business tour there and still remembered vividly the rough-surfaced crooked roads of that country. 'Real death-traps, those! And how you folks drive your automobiles! So crazy – why don't they clear those wrecks off the highways?' the travellers reminisced together.

But host and hostess, fearing a head-on collision between their two guests right there at the setting out, steered the conversation to educational publishing in Nigeria, the abiding subject of their mission to Africa and other dark places needing light. And the publisher president was full of questions for which he had himself all the answers. Like, what did I think of my country's novelists? They were a promising lot, weren't they? Oh, so I did think the novel was not African because it was a literate form and experienced only by the individual? Which meant I disapproved of all my colleagues! But seriously, didn't I agree that the elimination of English matter from our school syllabus would affect standards for the worse? It might be good politics, but that's not what he meant. His fear was that African students, history and English ones for example, going overseas, would no longer be at home with the subjects others were studying in the great universities. Yes, a start had to be made somewhere, but how was the balance to be preserved, and where to find the teachers able to put across the new material? And could I tell them where to find the authors for the new African histories and readers? It seemed to him the solution lay in the present syllabus for all its being colonial.

I had hardly touched my supper for arguing with the publisher. Now both husband and wife stepped in again and directed us to the safe course of the table, all superbly laid out by their Negro housekeeper, who threw me an anxious look now and again. Later they all took me back to the Graduate College, and for once I was glad to be back there, alone and unsolicited in my room.

At nearly all the large house parties I had invitations to, either from couples living in a perpetual state of unpack in tenement buildings, say in the deep lower and upper reaches of New York, or from career couples comfortably established in shiny, anonymous apartment blocks, as well as from upper middle class, middle-aged couples retired far away from the madding crowd in wooden-fronted suburban mansions, I always ended up right in the heart of a curious circle of guests asking this or that question about Africa and giving me that knowing quizzical look when I provided a piece of information quite contrary to the prototype image they had in mind. The tenement people showed a preference for the arty subjects and were more open and disinterested in discussing matters American.

On the other hand, the aspiring prospering professionals inclined to topics political or economics and sociology within their group. Conversation was often a criss-cross of comparisons and queries to the ding-dong tune of 'did-you-read-that?' and 'you-should-read-the-other-fellow: his-latest-work-is-a-sure-must.' With the propertied and the nouveau riche, usually ensconced away in self-contained communities, the pattern becomes even more interesting. First one accommodating man, armed with a glass of gin or some other firewater, ambles up and discloses a mind curious for geography. He takes a chair by me in one corner of the overdone and decorated lounge, and immediately another pulls up his seat to join in so that before we have left the realm of the flora and fauna of Africa, others have made a complete circle about us. How is the state of education down there? Nigeria has up to five colleges? Always thought the place no bigger than a penny-stamp on the map. And you have cities and civilizations long established before Columbus discovered us? Fancy that! Now, which of the presidents was shot recently? Oh, yes, aren't things a bit unstable there right now? You don't think so? In other words, you are saying foreign investment would be safe for a long time to come in the New Africa. Hm, the newspapers don't make it look so!

But the discussion, somewhat dry and impersonal before, inevitably turns to sex, love and marriage habits in other lands, that is, in Africa, as compared to the honourable, democratic practice of co-equal, loving partners observed among American couples. By this time however, the ladies in their silk and fineries, smelling a conspiracy of males against their dominance of the house, fan their way floatingly to form an outer ring to the group. Did they understand me to be offering defence for the obnoxious practice of polygamy, almost as vile as that other uncivilized practice of clitoridectomy? They flounce up to me.

'Oh, it isn't more so than circumcision,' say some men there taking up cudgels for me, and as several there are often Jewish the blow usually gets home.

'I don't understand at all!' A frothy-fronted lady stamps her plump foot.

'Oh, don't you, dear? Some surgeon fellow takes hold of

the clitoris and with one fell movement of hand, slices the offending thing off!' crows a successful merchant showing a medical turn of mind.

'How dreadful!' gulps every bejewelled throat craned forth.

'Oh, how wicked!'

'But it probably takes care of that itch in the promiscuous!' The oversatiated merchant guzzles down another drink.

'Still I don't see how I can share one man with another woman – Darling, that would be like allowing you other lovers!'

The women remain petulant together.

'Well, the fellow says his mother is quite happy with his father who has a dozen other wives,' the darling husbands assure them.

'O la la!' issues the universal whistle.

'And no two persons could be closer than my mother and father are,' I rub it in.

'How can that be?' The women rise in one voice.

'One man to several women deprives the wife of her rights!' they intone together.

'And what are those rights?' I laugh.

Surprisingly, there is a hush, for none there can think up immediately their famous well guaranteed rights. Until one, spirited and aloud, speaks of her co-equal rights to any property her husband has – like the home and his business. To this I say my mother has her self-contained apartment in the concession or compound and that she has her own farming, fishing, or independent trading to do when not helping with the larger business of the husband. And at her age, which probably is that of many of my fellow guests, she would be too concerned with the well-being of her children to go nervous and neurotic over sex as apparently is the pre-occupation of most American wives.

'Oh, that's not fair at all,' come the protests, frantic still but becoming decidedly abashed.

However, I do not give any quarter now. Oh, yes, I press on with my victory, in the old African set-up still intact outside the cities, women slept with their men usually only between their monthly periods. In other words, procreation was the first thought, not pleasure, which was incidental. Nine months the housewife was heavy with child, and another nine or more she weaned her child before there was thought of making another.

'Meanwhile, the man does his rounds with the others!' someone breaks into a high-pitched laugh and clap. 'A very sensible rotational system it seems to me. Old Solomon must have done just that! It carries its own birth-control safe and natural.'

'Yes, doesn't it all sound gorgeous for you men!'

'Well, I think most people are polyerotic anyway.'

'And I still think polygamy an obnoxious practice.'

'Oh, not so different from what the young man calls our serial system of marrying today only to divorce tomorrow to begin a long string of uncertain couplings.'

'That at least is a democratic process, and things are even between both parties.'

So ran the conversation at a typical big bourgeois house party I attended, everybody talking at the same time, not to advance the progress of anything but usually only so that each could score a point and not feel left out and without really having to listen to one another. The gentleman who had started it all with me earlier in the evening rose up at last to go home. 'Young man,' he held my hand, 'let me know when you are returning home. I sure want a holiday in Africa.' A short scattered burst of laughter as of expensive china broke uncomfortably down the room, for just then his wife, a roundish woman, who all evening had shown sparkling fire playing on a large piano at the other end of the spacious sitting-room, came by to collect her shawl and overcoat and handbag from where such costumes are usually deposited as opening to the night's ritual.

'You must be a happy man with such an accomplished pianist for a wife, to delight you every day at home,' I said awkwardly, the lady bowing graciously to my compliment.

'On the contrary, my boy,' her husband bade me good-night, 'the very fact that she is so good makes it all the more frustrating for everybody that she is not performing at Carnegie Hall.'

Then there was the usual bussing of cheeks and even lips and the brief exchange of hugs among neighbours, all very formal and rather chilling to the stranger, after which each guest and couple found their individual ways into the dark and cold outside with mutual calls of 'goodnight' and 'goodbye'.

Although I stopped with several American families at their kind invitation, I never quite gained a fair estimate of the size of circle of acquaintances my host families called friends. How large and constant is it? I sold the problem to a professor of sociology almost in my last dinner engagement at Princeton. A veritable encyclopaedia on the social life of his country, the surprise was that he did not quite know himself. A friend of his at Harvard had conducted a study like that before, and made the interesting find that any two Americans, that is, picked at random among any number of states, have friends whose friends know one another's friends. Which was not quite the same thing. Nor sense to anybody, snorted another professor present at our table. 'If it comes merely to knowing of people,' he pooh-poohed the whole theory, 'do you have to go to all that length? I know of Police Commissioner Bull O'Connor of Birmingham, because I have read of him and his dogs let loose on Negroes in the papers.'

There were of course house parties, but these told more what a household could offer by way of conspicuous consumption than who was a friend and who a business associate or rival one wanted to impress to some purpose and profit. A house, even more to the American than to the proverbial

Englishman, has become a castle, indeed, a cocoon. You drive out of it in your serpentine automobile because you have to go to work to pile up those dollars, to run the children to school if they are not to miss the opportunity of going to college, which is 'America's best friend', and you spend a night out of the house because you are taking the entire family for the year's holiday to some beach or outlandish country. So one gets cooped up there most of the time, especially during winter, like some dormouse in its hole. Fortunately, there is plenty of room for everybody to pad about and play inside. Daddy perhaps has the library and the tool or box-room to potter about in, the children have their nursery and toy-lobby which may take the whole under-carriage section of the house to accommodate a railway network, and of course Mummy who rules over all with great affection and firmness has her holy of holies, the kitchen.

A special creation here, the kitchen is one of America's three super graces. The others in that trinity are, the telephone always at your elbow, making it possible for you in New York to date and clinch a deal with another in California, and those vast, toll-collecting highways streaming away in multiple long stretches to the horizon, and which together with the millions of automobiles sweeping them in all directions of the wind, give rise to the old query: which came before the other, the egg or the chicken? But even more treasured and revered by all is the kitchen. With its refrigerator, cooker, washing-machine, dish-washer, crockery boards, chromium racks, and a hundred odd gadgets and ends, some for crushing and splicing, others for reforming and moulding meals which often are only half cooked to retain all calories and vitamins, the American housewife's kitchen, even more than nuclear stock-piles, has become the debate-winner for the United States in the ideological clash and Cold War since former Vice-President Richard Nixon had his famous culinary encounter with Nikita Kruschev.

With every member of the family in such good company and so well provided for, the home is world enough certainly to all. You can follow all the sports shows and news on a round-the-clock TV coverage, and there is always the telephone to make any call anyone can think of. So why go visiting? In any case, who actually bothers to come over, especially over the snowed-down impassable highways in winter? These conditions favour a closing together of ranks among members of the family. Consequently, parents and children, each denied the wider companionship of members of their own age group, become co-equal members of one close club, swapping jokes and ice-cream cones, and flinging things at each other on grown-up equal terms, a relationship I found at once most touching and disturbing.

Like the odd tug-of-war I witnessed at work within one American girl. When not placing orphans and juvenile delinquents in decent Christian homes or helping to mend broken homes and marriages, she was refurbishing old folk airs for records, and smoking marijuana.

'Haven't they got you on that yet at Princeton?' she tossed her head out of the fumes mushrooming about her, when I declined her loving offer of a drag.

7 · WANDERING SCHOLARS

African students had just suffered their brush-up in Sofia, and in the United States of America daily newspapers and magazines, from *Time* and the *New York Herald Tribune*, two of America's most rabid watchdogs, to the sedate and so-called liberal *New York Times* and *Post*, were all having a field day of it. The Communists are sure now having their comeuppance, they shrilled in one chorus of I-told-you-so and self-congratulation, and wasn't it great that Africans them-selves, long deceived and believing in the miracle of the new Red Saviour, should have kicked these wide chinks in the iron and bamboo walls of communism? Out of there, now pouring for all to see, were the ugly rank smoke clouds from the vast cauldron that is Communist-run countries! By far the most flavoursome and well-served-up of all the news stories was that by the newsmagazine *Newsweek*.

In a way, all this hysteria, typical of America, was a wonderful break, as the Press had all plunged after President Kennedy into the stewing pot of Cuba, and after six whole months of shouting curses and flailing arms, had none of them shown any stomach or grace for an honourable pull-out. Except that on my calling at the State Department early in

May I was offered, as must have been several foreign com-
municants all over the US at that time, the *Newsweek* stuff
as the new communion bread and wine.

'Oh, you read that report, did you?' The diplomat who
received me described a fresh circle on the blotting paper in
his front.

'Yes,' I said.

'Wasn't that pretty accurate and comprehensive of them?'
he drew another between his asking and my answer.

'Yes, if you are talking of the dating habits among the
several foreign students studying here, and of the long dis-
tances they do to come to rich Uncle Sam's.'

'Well, wasn't it dating behind those Sofia riots?' the
diplomat looked up at me, his pen held up on the incomplete
arc of an oncoming circle.

'A real shame, that,' I conceded, shifting in my seat. 'And
we have them here in surplus!'

'Poor fellows, now they have to find themselves fresh
places.'

'I thought the US had her ample arms open to receive the
prodigals and rejected?'

'Yes, that's true.' He brought yet another circle to happy
fruition. 'As a government however there is a limit to what
we can do openly. But private voluntary organizations and
individual citizens and colleges acting in their own behalf
and of their own free will are rising to this new challenge.
Now, that's the great thing about our system: everybody
acts as a completely free agent.'

I laughed out openly and rudely before he had finished.

'Now, you may not think it's so, but that's what we
Americans believe.' The quiet diplomat, who had now
dropped his pen on a blotter full of well-rounded circles,
refused to be ruffled by me. It had been an open and frank
discussion, not just as the jargon goes, and now I shoved
back my chair and rose to go, which brought the diplomat
up to his feet. He was tall and broad from feet to shoulders

as every American male should be, so that his shadow easily fell over me as he leaned over his desk. We reached across it to each other and shook hands. 'Look in on us any time you are in Washington DC,' he smiled warmly.

'Yes, I sure will,' I returned his firm grip. 'Especially if a cop clobbers me on the head.'

It was true what the man had said of private voluntary bodies and individual citizens taking up all on their own their country's constant, self-inflicted conflict with others of the world. Of course in these days of the Cold War, it is difficult to tell where cold calculating Greek gifts begin with the American people and when warm, altruistic Christian charity is at work with them. But that theirs is a faith well tried in action it would be a sin to deny. Even at Princeton so lily pure and preserved for the privileged, there exists now strong and positive evidence of America's dedication to the cause of helping the poor and oppressed of the world. Indeed the new pied beauty of the place resulting from the authentic appearance of black faces from the Congo, Nyasa and Nigeria has won for it a fresh virtue worthy to be sung. And much of the credit here as on other fronts and fields must go to such private associations of free citizens and good Samaritans like the American African Institute which incidentally and much to the surprise of many an educated American publishes a whole magazine on Africa every month.

Over the last three years, in a super drive to improve the supply of well-trained indigenous man-power for the independent states freely sprouting all over the dark African continent, the Institute has launched in close co-operation with the US Government at home and with participating governments abroad a crash programme to place in American colleges and universities African boys and girls of promise. As the slogan goes, never has so much been done by so few for so many and in so short a time. In Nigeria alone, for example, the Institute now air-lifts on the average every year a hundred or so students straight into dormitories and classes in the US. Without doubt, this is a bold and most worthy venture, and for the young starry-eyed Nigerians, the occasion, as Lagos newspaper men have liked reporting it since the doyen days of Dr Nnamdi Azikiwe, is like Jason setting forth once again in his relentless quest for the golden fleece.

The pity, however, is that these young men and women the Institute carries off every year to the States are some of the brightest products the few secondary grammer schools or senior high schools in the new countries of Africa have to offer the still fewer and newer home universities and colleges. Already, among African universities the cry is hoarse for a steady source of suitable student material that will keep them in constant supply. The situation therefore seems to be one of a lame dog being further crippled by the kind-hearted passer-by who wants to help him over the stile. The University of Ibadan, for example, has suffered this kind of awkward, unintentioned mauling at the hands of the American African Institute. My cousin at Princeton, for one, after a brilliant performance at his higher school certificate examination, had an open position at Ibadan to train as a medical doctor, the very kind of qualified men needed most in his Delta part of Nigeria. But what happened when it came to making the final choice? As a matter of fact, it seemed then there was not one to make. So overpowering and all-pervading was the siren call of America, that the young man, like several others who began the programme that year, fell for the offer, and so off he was swept to Princeton, the name of which he did not even know of at that time. Now he has taken a degree in chemistry, or is it biology? True, his is only a single case, but very likely representative of that first year, and indeed those following since. Who will ever know the true extent of such misdirections, the wandering astray, and the complete loss in the woods therefrom?

The danger and waste become greater still when guides and benefactors, as apparently these do-good American citizens and associations are, show little awareness of the problems involved, and worse still, refuse to admit their existence when they are pointed out to their all-seeing, radar, and X-ray eyes. And that they are most painstaking and conscientious over the welfare of each girl and boy they take across the seas to the States it would be churlish to deny for one moment. Wards each have a foster home and godparents. One boy I met made much of the fact that his white foster-mother kisses him every time he goes home to his adopted family. Another spoke of the care and effort his always took to arrange dates for him. One snag though, he admitted, and all of us there laughed long and loud, is that she would not have them a mixed affair! And there was the boy who said that the very thought of sitting through church services and retreats on Sundays spoiled for him the fun of going home to his otherwise very loving foster-family. These are all real problems, those of young people, and in a far-away place. That they are so well taken care of must in a large measure be the work and motherly solicitude of the American upper-middle class housewife, a common force on all such committees.

Other problems however, perhaps less personal, remain unattended or simply ignored. Take that of post-graduate studies, which is the dream of the American student. It not only puts him in a class but he also needs his second degree or doctorate to expect a place on the faculty in most universities or even in corporations or the civil service outside. Because the various authorities and grant donors fully own up to their responsibilities of making money, men and equipment available for the task of staffing industry and society with higher cadres of personnel, the average intelligent American youth can expect to go beyond his bachelor's degree as a matter of course.

Apparently, however, it is not so with the African student sponsored by educational organizations like the American African Institute. 'What do you want to do graduate work for?'

they frown at applicants for extension of grants. 'Africa needs first degree men, not scholars!' As likely as not, the idea of hurrying home African graduates carries a lot of sense, since the poor old folks at home require instant basic services. But Africa also requires now the secondary ones. With careful planning and acceleration where the potential exists, it should be possible to combine both needs with profit for all. It seems therefore criminal negligence to deny students with aptitude, and call off their one opportunity to develop themselves fully first before going out to develop others. Further, partly due to superior attitudes taken over by Africans from their imperial masters and partly in real recognition of the fact, the first American college degree in Africa is regarded even now with great suspicion. And in this probably unequal discrimination no distinction is made as between Harvard and Howard.

Indeed, Americans themselves subscribe and contribute to this. I once had an American graduate student in an English class repeat to me, almost apologetically, that he came down from Haverford in the State of Pennsylvania, and not Harvard! The special anxiety of African students in America must therefore be placed in proper perspective to be appreciated. None wants to return home with just the first diploma, and indeed they would be refused responsible appointments by their own governments today, as did the British colonial governments many years ago when they snubbed scholars like Dr Azikiwe and his American-educated contemporaries. This imperial relic has dug its roots so deep among public service boards in Nigeria, the story goes that even a young graduate from the Massachusetts Institute of Technology was passed over for a job since no expert there could place his qualifications!

But distinctions there certainly are, and these have to be insisted upon all the time, if the gates are not going to be sluiced and soiled water let through in a rush to flood everybody out. The programme for the mass placement of African students in colleges in the United States of America seems at the moment to be courting just this disaster. Those floating it, with all the good intentions in the world, are today increasing its area of participation. Consequently, the programme now flows over from the Ivy League colleges which began it to all sorts of colleges all across the United States. The idea of course is to increase output in the quickest possible time. In the drive towards quantity however the tendency towards a lowering in quality and standards cannot be regarded as a mere bugaboo. Not that anybody is saying the new expanding network of colleges to which students are now being drafted all lack proper accreditation. It is just that, as in the animal farm, some members prove more equal than others, and when all must eventually return to render equal service where distinction and discrimination are rife, it is only fair that right from the start opportunities are not made free to the exclusive advantage of one sector.

At this point, one may venture to question the courses of study many of these students find themselves pursuing. For instance, it can be safely asked what a Nigerian goes all the way to America to learn of the arts that he cannot readily do at a university back home. If he is a history man, and very possibly taking classes in the witch-hunt sessions of Boston during Colonial days, of what value and practical use can this be to him and his society? The acquiring of knowledge and a complete kit quick to reach for purposes of comparison and critical application is an essential aim of every true scholar, but of what relevance and use is the plucking of such lush leaves outside when the yam underground in the concession at home is there still to uproot? Without being parochial and short-sighted, one can at least try starting the practice of charity at home!

As with the arts so to some extent with the sciences. Here the real snag is not so much that a good physics laboratory in Lagos should satisfy the same basic teaching needs and conditions that obtain in New York and Moscow, as the

more awkward, if less obtrusive one of students picking up
skills and tricks for which there appears no immediate
audience and provision at home. I knew of a young Nigerian
engineer who went from Ohio to pursue a further course in
plastics at Princeton. Naturally, he required some extra funds
to realize this end. So he went straight to the Nigerian
ambassador in Washington, who was gracious and kind
enough to arrange for him an audience with the Premier of his
region who happened then to be around in the US on one of
those begging bouts officiously called economic missions
abroad. 'What do you want that for anyway?' the Premier
scolded him. 'Yes, what is this you say you want an extension
of scholarship for? Young man, there is no industry like that
at home, and if I may let you into a secret nobody is planning
one!' The follow-up of this cordial meeting was an urgent
trans-Atlantic summons a few days afterwards, ordering the
young engineer to return home by the next plane.

But by far the most absurd of all the educational schemes
for Africa now emanating from America and elsewhere
appears to be that with which President Kennedy himself and
his clan have direct and personal interests and connection.
I do not mean the official Peace Corps programme which for
all the selfish indirect gains the US Government expects to
reap out of it at the expense of the Soviet Union, and which
for all the callowness, bad-equipment and escapist tendencies
of a good number of its draftees and volunteers, has proved
itself an original, unique enterprise now crying to be applied
to blighted sectors of the home front itself. The absurd
schemes I have here in mind are those which, conceived in
the mistaken notion of beginning at the grass-roots level, aim
at attracting to America boys and girls still very much in their
early formative years. In this misguided belief, wealthy
American families, like that of the Kennedy clan, working in so-
called partnership with African politicians, like Tom Mboya,
ready to do anything for the education of their people, have
actually in the last few years air-lifted hundreds of mere

children from Kenya to attend high schools in the United States. Starting right from scratch, it is expected that these kids will pass through the special preparatory schools that are concomitant with the exclusive system into which they have been thrown like flies on to a spider's web, and go on from there to even more selective colleges fed from these schools. For each child, this may take anything from ten to fifteen years of grooming so that by the time he is passed out fit to return home to serve his people he has become a better Yankee than a Kikuyu.

Instead of spending so much money and time on breeding a rank plant of alienation and waste, would it not pay more dividends to all if the public-spirited promoters behind these ventures provided part or whole of the money and men to open and staff new schools and colleges right in those countries needing development of their abundant raw material ? The operation would certainly cost less in terms of effort and funds, and far from ill-preparing a select group for service, it should reach a greater number of the people and a much wider area of the country in which they live and die.

Incidentally, this is an approach that can well be adopted for the direct college projects both at the undergraduate and research levels. Five universities serving Nigeria's 40 million people is not exactly excellent service. But when there appears lacking an adequate under-carriage of secondary schools to support that structure, and when this actually yields less than two thousand school leavers every year capable, as they say, of benefiting from a university education, then there is every cause to worry over the lure to the United States and to Europe of some of the best brains Nigeria has to offer her already starving universities.

Now to those who know all this there is a terrible irony. For only a few years ago, before the University of Ibadan was founded, everybody, bright and dull, once the funds and drive were there, went overseas to seek the Golden Fleece. But as soon as Ibadan got under way, it became evident that she was attracting to herself a growing majority of the best material available from the schools. Indeed, but for a few affluent ones, and some others who as a result of bad co-ordination and poor policy on the part of government still won bursaries to go abroad, Ibadan in a matter of a few years had come to absorb almost all of the best, so that there grew the rather cruel joke that those who still went abroad for courses available at home were rejects of Ibadan! But to return to our bright ones abroad now, I saw a fair sprinkling of these boys and girls at Princeton, Harvard, Barnard and Cornell. Now that the initial gloss has worn off, the general opinion among them was, 'wouldn't it have been wonderful to go to Ibadan and then perhaps come over here for research work!' Boarding and tuition fees between these top US universities range in the 3,000 to 5,000 dollar bracket a year for a single student. This will more than take care of the entire course for the undergraduate at Ibadan, and in fact, for another or two others at Nsukka and Zaria.

In other words, if an American benefactor of Africa, like the American African Institute or the Kennedy Family Foundation, will raise all the money they are now doing and come into understanding with the African governments who pay only the passage fares to and fro for the students, all the vast resources now being lavished on a few abroad, who are getting increasingly fed up, can be put fully to use on the fallow, fertile field itself, and to the greatest advantage of everybody seeking proper cultivation of it.

And even on the research side, the land needs a closer examination if further exploiting of it is to bear fresh fruit. At Cornell and Toronto, for example, I discovered old friends and colleagues at home, doing their second degrees in English. It seemed however that quite apart from the theoretical and technical aspect of their course, which was training them to become university teachers, a good portion of the papers they had to offer were no further advance from the period and special papers they had done already for their first degrees. 'What have you to offer at home? You people are only beginning to write. Here we are studying American Literature,' one protested to me vigorously.

'To do what with?' I insisted.

'To teach of course. Or do you disapprove of Emerson as a transcendentalist?'

'You mean at home in Nigeria?'

'Tell me where else.'

'Well, I guess the right place to teach American Literature would be in US schools.'

'Nonsense, and you a writer! Aren't you being parochial?'

'Oh, no; in point of fact I'd very much rather you went to Moscow or Tokyo.' And I think I said something to the effect that English students like him were but poor products of sterile professors still propping up private outposts for themselves while the Empire was fast falling apart around everybody, and that it was the peculiar warped opinion of those initiated in this obsolescent school and cult to forget that oral literature has as much legitimate life as that hawked between two inscribed covers. My friend looked me up and down and asked whether I was just being facetious or plain jealous. I promptly denied the charge on both counts.

'Then it is world comparative literature you must be thinking of?' he mused wisely.

I said perhaps. By this time however we had attracted quite a lot of attention from indigenous students and faculty members shunting their various ways to and from the university library at Toronto.

'Here,' someone pulled me round; 'why not come up to the Common Room, and then we can all discuss this over a cup of coffee? You are right in the middle of the street here, you know.'

And so we were. Our new friend and moderator, when he finally came into focus, turned out to be a postgraduate student from Bombay, and although he proved interesting at table and talked as sweetly of the international character of

F

letters as he did bitterly of standards falling in his native India, the heat had gone out of us all there, so that the coffee went cold in my hands, and I was glad when someone reminded me of another engagement long since overdue.

Nor was it among English students alone that there was this vague sense of misdirection and drift, and the often attendant defensive stance, touchy and bristling at the least sign of attack. My host in Toronto, who was a history graduate from home, had completed his master's degree with a study of how Australia had fulfilled the mandate the United Nations gave her over New Guinea. Now all set for his doctorate on some aspect of his own country's political career, he finds he has either to go on flying down across the border to the Library of Congress in Washington which hasn't got all the documents anyway, or come back home where the *West African Pilot* and *Daily Times* he needs so much for his material are published.

'Haven't I travelled some distance to arrive home!' he laughed in his direct, open manner. 'In the meantime,' he added, 'others from abroad are digging deep at home.'

'Oh, no,' I got infected by his laugh, 'of course they aren't; but don't you dare come home and call them squatters!'

Truly, as Dr Johnson put it so well on another occasion, not so different from ours, the Scythians wandered abroad to make conquest of the world; meanwhile strangers were in occupation of Scythia.

8 · ATOP CAPITOL HILL

On a Decision Day in January, members of the Parvin Fellowship Programme, appropriately led by their director Colonel Robert Van de Velde, paid a visit to the United States Supreme Court as personal guests of Associate Judge William O. Douglas. Characteristically, I had arrived late that Monday morning, although Mimi Crowell, as lovable a hostess as she was formidable and stimulating in talk, especially when establishing her claim that Americans are altruistic by nature, had taken the extra trouble of driving me into town herself. So, as I climbed the high steps to justice, official frowns lowered upon me. I had just enough time to check my topcoat before tailing the group, all on its best behaviour now, into the vast crowded hall of the Supreme Court of the United States of America.

Quite a number of attorneys from a sprinkling of states were getting enrolled that day and we had to sit through their long repetitious ceremony of oath-taking. That tedium plus the fact that there in the spacious precincts of the court were some of the surest nuclear blast shelters, not only in the Union but in all the universe, gave me such a settled and safe feeling at last that I had quite a job, without at all wanting to

be disrespectful, of staying wide awake through the proceedings of the court, ultimate across the wide sweep of the
land. My alarm therefore was great and genuine when a bull-
dog faced usher or marshal lumbered up to where we Parvin
people sat as a group and said throatily: 'Stay awake there!'
But I need not have jumped out of my skin. 'Yes, you, madam,'
the muscular arm of the law seized upon his quarry, 'you stay
awake or step out with me.' It was Barbara, the Colonel's
own wife, sitting just next to me: I could not believe it.
Naturally the lady tried protesting vocally and vigorously in
the very democratic manner of her country but the marshal,
in equal defence of the Constitution, hushed her down and
then drew away to continue his beat. Meanwhile, too
embarrassed to look Barbara in the face, I took up study
of the sitting arrangement of the nine worthies on the
rostrum.

Right in the centre sat Chief Justice Earl Warren. Immediately to his left and right were our own Justice Douglas
and Justice Hugo L. Black, both of the so-called 'liberal'
group of the Court, and next to them as if to restore the
balance came the 'conservatives' Justice John M. Harlan and
Justice Tom C. Clark. Others to the right were the 'liberal'
Justice William J. Brennan Jnr and Justice Byron R. White
whose voting role was still to emerge, while at the opposite
end sat Justice Potter Stewart, often called the 'pivotal' man
between the 'liberal' and the 'conservative' voting blocs of
the Court, and last but by no means the least was Mr Justice
Goldberg who was the replacement for Justice Felix Frank-
furter, the much feared old interrogator of counsel, now
retired. All fitted-out in gowns, they presented a fine group
portrait of white in black, and as about half of them persistently
swayed forward and back in their rocking chairs, just like the
President at his news conferences, while their colleagues
remained immobile in their solid seats of oak, I had the
strange feeling of being before some frightening flank or
phalanx, not quite advancing, not quite receding for any

appreciable length of time, like waves upon the shore.

The Court handed down three decisions that morning, one agreeing with the claims of a Chinese American in California that the police in their investigations of a certain dope racket had trampled brutally on the man's fundamental human rights as a citizen of the US. A second ruling, concerning two petrol dealers, one of whom had succumbed to cut-throat competition with the other in spite of concessions obtained direct from his refinery and suppliers, established the fact that all is fair in war as in love. And the third judgment that session, one of personal interest to me and other black people there, was the Court's ruling in favour of the National Association for the Advancement of Coloured People to the effect that a party other than that directly aggrieved had every right under the Constitution of the United States to concern itself with seeking on behalf and in concert with the aggrieved a redress for the abuse of his rights as a citizen. This in its own way was a decision great enough to stand beside the famous Brown v. Board of Education of Topeca, Kansas desegregation decision in 1954, and the Baker v. Carr ruling in 1962, conceding voters their right to sue in federal courts if deprived of equal representation through state devices such as malapportionment.

An additional duty performed, among many others most onerous, by each Justice of the Court is a personal hearing of applications for bails and stays of various sentences. Justice Douglas, I was told, enjoyed the fine reputation of attracting the majority of these frantic, desperate calls for rescue directed at him, giving to each a most sympathetic hearing. At the close of the session, the old judge, as responsive as ever to calls by applicants of all sorts for his personal attention, took us of the Parvin Programme, over which he presides, into a reception room in his chambers where he treated us to cocktails. For a man of his age and position, the judge proved jaunty, spontaneous and communicative beyond belief. Glass in hand, he breezed among his guests from several lands, and being much travelled and read, showed himself at ease and home with each.

'You are a writer, I hear,' he cornered me. 'Then we are of the same profession. Have you seen my new book?'

'You mean *America Challenged*? I enjoyed reading it very much.'

'Thank you; but that's my old one. I meant the new book I have just brought out. I call it *Manifesto for Democracy*.'

'No, I haven't seen it yet.'

'Then I must have a copy mailed to you immediately, all of you in fact.'

'Is your book, Sir, a reply to the *Communist Manifesto*? my Polish friend Daniel Passent asked with a laugh.

'Don't ask me,' the old judge winked an eye. 'I'm holding brief for nobody, and making a reply to none either. But I believe there are positive virtues in the democratic way of life which nobody as yet has bothered to present in a manifesto the ordinary man can find winning and useful. And that's all I have tried to do.'

Next the old judge graciously posed for a photograph with us, keeping everybody talking and laughing all the time so that the photographer did not have to say cheese to get his smiles. After which our host turned to all of us and apologised that he would unfortunately not be at lunch with us, since the President was giving Congress that afternoon his state-of-the-union message, and Supreme Court Justices, as honourable members of the tripartite power, had all to be there. But other distinguished colleagues of his, representative of the entire judicial structure of the United States, would be pleased to dine with us and answer any queries we cared to voice. If he could, he would love to come back and rejoin the group, but if not, then this must be his parting with us Parvin Fellows, although we would always stay together in the spirit of open communication that engendered the programme. It was only after the learned judge had left us that I noticed we had not had the benefit of being presented to his wife. 'Where is Mrs Douglas?' I asked in all innocence. 'She suffered a bad accident recently and is still convalescing,' Colonel Van de Velde and his wife answered in one soothing voice. Later I heard of talk about separation and divorce, that the judge was to be married a third time, to a co-ed just graduated, and the wife was to be married for the second time, to a luminary of the Washington DC bar.

But to turn to those distinguished members of the American bench and bar present with us Parvins at that Douglas luncheon, I remember vividly the Chief Justice from the Circuit of Federal Appellate Courts, a judge at the Federal capital's own district court who had the rare distinction of being a three-term Governor of Minnesota, a newly appointed federal attorney with the asset of being the son of Dean Acheson, then the talk of the town for throwing the British a few home truths, which they thought insults. There was another attorney who said he acted as a filter and strainer in the Office of the President, and a veteran lawyer who had represented the United States on a number of high-powered committees in the United Nations. I sat by this remarkable old gentleman. He had a creeping bore-through-the-other-man's-body drawl that I still cannot track down now with any degree of precision as to his age or Yankee origin. And the Congo was a big bee in his bonnet, more bothering by its buzz than in its sting.

'I still do not think it is right for the United Nations to coerce Tshombe into returning Katanga to the rest of the Congo,' he told me for the umpteenth time.

'Why?' I blew my soup.

'Because Tshombe and Katanga ought to be conceded their individual sovereign right of choice,' he patiently explained to me.

'Just as Abraham Lincoln should have allowed the Confederate States to back out of the Union?' I blew my soup a trifle more.

'That's not a similar case at all,' the old man dropped his

spoon. 'The United States was already one country – '

'And the Congo?' I cut in.

'Whereas the Congo has never been,' the man ignored my rude interruption.

'Of course that's not true,' I said.

'Of course it is,' he corrected me. 'The Congo as you understand it was a mere creation of the Belgians out of several different tribes.'

'So some of us understood America to be – a creation of the British.'

I do not know how the matter could have ended had those post-prandial speeches not started then, and douched everybody with praise overflowing for the US judicial set-up and all that. Proposing the toast was the some time, many-term Governor now turned Judge. He must have taken his assignment more as an old-time politician than anything else, for he warmed into his part so much that he made a speech lasting the better part of an hour or more. And his theme was all one of greatness for America, especially after seeing in his world tour, brought only recently to a happy return home, how small all other systems were in comparison. By the time the feast was over I felt so sick I got up and threw out a query. This I was told in no uncertain terms afterwards was tantamount to contempt of court. And according to information volunteered by the Colonel later in our last encounter, he wanted to ship me home there and then on the one count of that misdemeanour, but Barbara his wife had pleaded for one more chance for me.

And my point had been that if we took the entire judicial structure of the United States as one tall tree, nobody would dispute the fact that the Supreme Court as the tree's crowning boughs and foliage was straining all the time to reach the sun, enjoying in the process its own fair amount of light and a high view which kept it in constant sight of climbers and spectators all over the world. But at the bottom base of the tree is the complex of police, justice of peace, municipal, county, state courts, and it is within the close, oppressive shadow of these that the majority of citizens walk, get trampled upon, and must seek shelter and refuge.

Only a very small handful possess the extra energy, skill and expensive equipment, not to mention the courage and patience essential for scaling the stout and tall tree to attain for themselves justice at the top. But what happens to the bulk of people below? The situation becomes even more dangerous when those entrusted to tend the tree at the base are men and women, not necessarily the brightest independent minds a community has to offer, but are mostly career politicians voted into office at popular heady elections held on partisan party lines. Thus the entire line-up, from the prosecutor to the magistrate and judge, consists of party functionaries put in office on the same ticket that determines the election of governors, representatives and Senators. And assisting them in arriving at decisions day by day are the normal and grand juries picked and summoned out of a standing list of responsible respectable citizens.

Of course all this is a fair reflection of the democratic way of life as Americans have lived it since George Washington booted out the English, and the astounding achievement of it has been that exemplary spirit of a people bred on the ideals of individual freedom. But what happens if, as was disclosed by a rare defending attorney to the shock of America, the entire staff tending the tree are drawn, and indeed have always been and will for a long time to come, exclusively from one sector of an irrevocably mixed community, even though the cry is that all offenders come of that one neglected section called coloured? Could the accused ever expect a fair trial and sentence for a charge often as flimsy and trumped up by bitter and frustrated members of the dominant sector? The answer has been lived down through a century of lynchings and compliance to the will of mob-rule, and only lately many all over the United States must have found it distressing on seeing the film *To Kill a Mockingbird*.

That was a long-winded and florid query, put almost exactly in the foregoing words and imagery. I am happy to report that it got a very terse and brief reply. The matter of tyrannies and atrocities to the individual was one for education, the Chief Justice pronounced ruling, and the government and the people of the United States were doing the very best they could. At this point, with all eyes balefully and pitifully focussed on me where I had slumped back into my seat, I did not dare ask whether those two in happy concert, the American government and people, included the Negro as well.

A most beautiful and very mysterious lady, insured for millions of dollars and guarded closely by battalions of police and soldiers, was then in Washington on a royal tour of America from Europe. Millions had already paid court to her before her imminent sweep off to New York. Her name? Mona Lisa. 'Shall we all go and see her as we do the city?' asked the charming guide who had come with us from the Foreign Student Service Council in their unpretentious centre almost opposite the White House.

'Count me out,' I said ungallantly and at that everybody looked at me without an ounce of Christian forgiveness in their eyes.

'Oh, Mr Clark knows his way around and has more interesting friends to see.' Barbara Van de Velde put it all very neatly, and I knew I was lost for ever.

For the Parvin Group the following day was Senate and House of Representatives Day. I was late again, although Eldon Crowell had let me in very early from my late night outing, and Mimi had again taken the extra care of running me from her Georgia suburb district to Capitol Hill. So there was a terrible show of temper and official frowning when I reported at the office of Representative Frank Thompson, a Democrat from New Jersey. He had already finished briefing his guests about the job of being a Congressman when I arrived. Since nobody around exactly approved of my late arrivals, all we had was a brief exchange of greetings. Which was double loss to me, having before at Princeton missed seeing Representative Thompson, then a candidate seeking re-election to Congress, make a snowball of his rival at a public debate sponsored by the League of American Women Voters. All I could therefore admire of the man was the complete secretarial service and large office facilities he enjoyed as of right with other Congressmen.

In Westminster and Lagos, I recalled, Members of Parliament have to file up behind one another to dictate letters to joint hands at a common typing pool. For them, pennies for stamps to answer irate letters from one constituent or another totalled up to a pretty tall bill, whereas a Congressman merely had to frank his mail and it was as good as the Treasury Seal. The one damper to the occasion was the fact that I could not help admitting to myself, more so as we entered deeper into the heart of the establishment, that America really is a white country, with blacks merely there on terms worse than sufferance. For walking from members' offices through the endless corridors to the close committee rooms and more or less empty halls, all with paintings and photographs of America's past and present great presidents and parliamentarians proudly mounted on their walls, I looked out steadily for a black face among that vast concourse of Congressmen and their staff, but had not the good fortune of running into one.

As we left at last to catch up with our tight and tedious schedule, Mr Thompson's personal assistant or secretary announced to me that somebody wanted me on the telephone. I could not readily think of anyone who would page me there, but Barbara knew already even before I picked up the receiver: 'Oh, some of his smart set!' she said, and everybody laughed. It turned out, however, to be some lobby correspondent or worse sponge wanting to report back home to the chain of newspapers that kept him in hire in the federal hive. He had heard that I was there, a fellow newspaper man, with another from Poland, and could we tell him what we thought of the US and of Congress in particular, now that we had visited it. For once I did not fly off the handle but had the sense to stall and soft pedal, eventually being rescued by Barbara and two other ladies who came along as gracious guides from the International Visitors Information Service. 'Come on, we must be going!' they shooed me out. And that done, they were hot with questions: 'Who was that calling? What did you tell him?'

'Oh, nobody or anything special,' I poured cold water on them.

'Really?' they shrilled together. 'Well, the man is in a hell of a mood this morning.'

The party moved straight from there to the Senate building, not without first going on a merry-go-round type of trolley train shunting passengers to and fro underground across the streets above. After such pains and expectations it was not a particularly impressive meeting of the Senators of America we saw that day on slipping into our seats in the visitors' gallery. Apparently nobody was sure of a quorum. So a roll-call or something had to be taken. None of those few distinguished personages directly involved in the matter seemed to pay much attention, however. But unmistakably present for all to see was the ultra-dyed-in-the-blue Conservative and Republican Senator Barry Goldwater with his clear American conscience right on his sleeve for all Yankees to view as a sure Presidential prospect. Also there was young Senator Edward Kennedy fresh from Boston in Massachusetts to complete, as he quipped like a proud junior to a dazzled coterie of bejewelled hostesses, the family picture in Washington DC. Minority Leader Senator Everett Dirksen, the veteran spell-binding orator from Illinois, was another distinguished figure I did not miss in the sparsely-populated gallery. At the height of Congress Elections combined with that of the Cuba Crisis, I remembered vaguely, he valiantly apropos of nothing spiced a speech of his with memories of some happy meeting he had had with either the President of Nigeria, then still not appointed, or the Prime Minister of Ghana!

One or two Russian graduate exchange students at Princeton (they never travelled outside a radius of seventy miles except with special permission from the State Department) had come to join our group. Apparently, the proceedings in the vast echoing hall below did not impress them much.

'Not at all like our Supreme Soviet,' they smiled. 'We are much too serious.' And later outside, on our way to lunch at the Methodist Building, close by the place where the great prohibition onslaught on America's drunken habits was launched and won for a short time in the thirties, Dan Passent, the Polish Parvin, had a more open laugh: 'Now, he said, 'we know where power actually lies in the United States!' The Colonel and his wife did not like this at all; nor naturally their co-patriots acting together as hosts and guides. So immediately the group returned to the grand tour, with a first and major stop at the offices of Senator Harrison Williams, the Colonel summoned all of us together behind closed doors, and gave us a good talking-to about the intricate, almost God-ordained, system of the US which is a strict, judicious one of checks and balances, between the three arms of government on the one hand, and on the other between the government and citizens of America, a people, some of us may not know or care to acknowledge, that are the fiercest in the fight for individual freedom and opportunity, unlike in other lands where millions live like cattle behind iron and bamboo fencings. In any case, their system, contrary to the criticism that it is run by a handful of men with all the money and power, has served them for hundreds of years of prosperity before or since then unknown to man elsewhere on the globe, and if some of us there did not know already, he would venture to mention that the American people have suffered no change of régime for more than a century and indeed were enjoying the most ancient government in the world with the monarchy in Britain possibly excepted.

Altogether the Colonel made a capital job of it, what with the surprise manner in which he sprang that briefing on us, not to mention its deep sincerity of voice and respect for facts. His colleague, usually more accommodating, also gave a little speech but coming after the Colonel's, his was an anticlimax with a very sharp 'i' as only Americans themselves know how to call it.

Only the entrance of Senator Harrison Williams, another Democrat from New Jersey, broke the tension of the meeting, and although he did not know it, he saved everybody a further dress-down and worse. Freshly returned from some Parliamentarian Conference in Lagos, he was full of praise for Nigeria and the international trade fair she had mounted while he was there. His one regret however, he chuckled in his baritone voice, was the terrible crush to get inside for the Ghana-Nigeria Soccer match played in Lagos. 'But it was sure great fun,' he assured me. Such was the warm, personal way the Senator handled each guest. And when a young colleague of his just elected from Dakota or some far out mid-west State came in to pay a courtesy call with many a 'Sir' and 'my Senior', he introduced him to us, and after more pleasantries saw us all to the door, shaking and waving hands all the time.

The group called on several more Congressmen as each asked that we look up his honourable friend at the next corner for another hard sell, but the one other stop that day I recall now was our visit to a Senate Committee hearing on some medical matter. I am not certain if it was not an aspect of the famous Medicare Bill itself. Anyway, it was a most crowded and heated affair, the Senators impanelled at one end of the hall, the interested lobby groups and members in the middle floor, and herded behind, close to the wall and doorway, sat and stood members of the general public, jostling and whisking past one another for space and every available seat. Cluttered in the midst of all this was a battery of audio-visual and public address equipment with cables all littered around, and cameras and film screens flashing now and again as a very high-powered delegation from the doctors put across their case.

For the way groups can persuade the American legislative system there is no better description than that offered voluntarily and proudly by the American National Theater and Academy in their brochure. I take the liberty to quote it in all its full length: 'A Federal Charter is not granted lightly,' the account opens grandly. 'In the history of the Congress of the United States, only a very few Congressional Charters have been granted to worthy organizations. This distinguished roster includes only one organization devoted to the theater arts: ANTA, the American National Theater and Academy.

'Years of complex negotiation lie behind ANTA's struggle for Congressional recognition which began at a quiet luncheon one day in November 1932. Mrs Amory Hare Hutchinson and Miss Mary Stewart French were discussing a new theatre project in Philadelphia and, from this meeting came the conviction that these plans could effectively be converted into a national theater organization, complete with Congressional Charter. With the cooperation of J. Howard Reber and Miss Clara Mason, the idea was first presented to President and Mrs Franklin D. Roosevelt at Hyde Park in August 1933. Mr Reber drew up a prospectus according to the President's enthusiastic suggestions. Support and interest began to widen. Largely through Mr Francis Crane's personal friendship with the President, a second interview with him at the White House in February 1934 was successful in obtaining his support for the ANTA Charter, as opposed to various other similar projects which were being discussed in Congress at that time. Further appointments with Secretary of Labor, Miss Frances Perkins, and Secretary of the Interior, Harold L. Ickes, helped to develop a plan of 'incorporators' – a small sponsoring group of about forty-five people, representing all national theater interests, but individually well-known as patrons of the arts. But it was not until a small White House luncheon on April 25, 1934, that official administrative assistance was definitely promised.

'Late the preceding fall, Miss Blanche Yurka who had been deeply interested in the idea of an American National Theater, was returning to Europe on the same ship with Senator Robert F. Wagner of New York. She so impressed him with the importance of the bill that he not only pledged his enthusiastic help – he further agreed to introduce the bill in the Senate. He was as good as his word. On April 22, 1935, 'S. 2642' – the bill proposing the incorporation and chartering of the ANTA – was presented by Senator Wagner to the Upper House.

'More than a month of steady Senate opposition served only to spur the unceasing efforts of Senator Wagner and Mary Stewart French, who had even taken up residence in Washington to be on hand for the fight. The cooperation of both labor and craft unions was enlisted. Conferences with Frank Gilmore, President of Actors' Equity Association, and William Green, President of the American Federation of Labor, brought invaluable assistance. Mr Green, who had signed the application for the Charter, and Mr Gilmore wired and wrote countless exhortations for support to influential members of both Houses of Congress. After several long and earnest conferences with Senator William H. King of Utah, leader of the Senate opposition, Senator Wagner was able to convince him of the importance and necessity for such an organization as proposed in his bill. Eventually, Senator King withdrew his arguments and, on May 28, 1935, the bill was passed by the Senate. The first battle was won!

'Representative Charles F. McLaughlin of Nebraska

agreed to present the bill to the House of Representatives and, a few days later, H.R. 8214 was introduced. Difficulties and delays began in earnest. The bill was resting in the hands of the Judiciary Committee, whose Chairman, Representative Hatton W. Sumners of Texas, vigorously opposed its approval.

'At a special hearing before Representative Sumners in June, a group of distinguished supporters spoke ardently in favour of the bill. Impassioned pleas were made by Representative McLaughlin, Miss Frances Starr (representing Actors' Equity Association), Mr Hushing (Legislative Representative of the American Federation of Labor), the Honourable Frederick Delano, uncle of the President and earnest worker for ANTA, and a host of others. Additional and unexpected opposition appeared when Representative William I. Sirovitch of New York testified that its passage would interfere with his own bill to found a Department of Science, Art and Literature. At the next meeting of the House Judiciary Committee a few days later, the Committee ruled against Representative Sirovitch and the bill was brought out of the Committee and placed on the House Unanimous Consent Calendar. Twice its passage was blocked by Sirovitch or his friends. Finally, a special rule was obtained from Congressman John J. O'Connor of New York, Chairman of the Rules Committee, allowing the bill to come up at any time and not just on a calendar day. On Saturday afternoon, June 29, Congressman McLaughlin was recognized by Speaker and, after a short debate on the floor of the House, 'H.R. 8214' was passed. The bill was signed by Speaker Burns for the House of Representatives and by Vice-President John Nance Garner for the Senate.

'On July 5, 1935, the formal bill incorporating the American National Theater and Academy was signed by the President of the United States, and ANTA was officially recognized.'

So ends the epic and saga of one pressure group. It carries

its own comment, and all we can say after is that God help
that American cause without the right type of connections
and resources. Against this backdrop the tragedy of the
Negro cause comes nakedly across the footlights.

Lobbies range from the country's most powerful and
influential business and Brahmin groups, like the American
Bankers Association, the Chamber of Commerce of the US,
the National Association of Manufacturers, and professional
propertied guilds like the American Medical Association that
is ensuring the death of free state medical care for the old,
all acting in their own behalf and interest, to private public
relations companies and individuals in the employ of South
American dictators and · Oriental tyrants, many of them
financed to begin with by the American tax-payer.

In 1962 alone as many as 367 new lobbies and agents
officially registered at both Houses of Congress, that is,
at the rate of one per day of the leap year, a sure sign of a
going business! Nor are all subtle and velvet-gloved like
ANTA. Indeed the operational methods the American
Federation of Labor – Congress of Industrial Organizations
uses for pushing its points up Capitol Hill can be quite drastic,
if not actually crude and full of the bludgeon of the bully or
apprentice. Representing some eighteen million white
workers and spending some one million dollars on TV time
a year, the organization, despite the somewhat churlish
image it cuts in the press, really is no underdog on the American cockpit of dog-eat-dog. It has a full-time staff of 21,000
enjoying the ideal of a five-and-a-half hour day in a five day
week, a minimum weekly pay of $103, and free health services
extended fully to the family.

So although feeling not a little deserted by white-collar
employees, and harassed by farmers, self-employeds, state
laws, an unemployment rate amounting to nearly six million
in the world's most prosperous country, and a division of
workers by colour and not skill, the labour movement in
America can tread pretty heavily on the feet of any politician

or businessman who crosses its path. The spokesman who addressed the Parvin party on our second official visit to Washington was most emphatic about this, his broad Milwaukee brogue serving very well to underline his point. The Kennedy-Nixon race for the presidency, he told us, offered a case of union action. Politics was not their business; all they did was adopt a fundamental, rule-of-thumb policy of reward for a friend and punishment for the enemy. And how did they decide who was which ? 'Simple,' he said. 'The labour unionists called for the Congressional records of both candidates and compared the individual performances of the junior Senator from Massachusetts and the Vice-President, who by virtue of his office presided over the Senate. Not on their overall showing, but how they debated and eventually voted in matters of labour and public welfare. By a simple chalking-off and head-counting process they were soon able to tell how many times one candidate was with them, and the other against them. And Kennedy emerged an easy winner.'

True to their true primitive heart, they proceeded straightaway to reward the one and to punish the other. A telephone call to one union member in this factory and a wire to this executive in that local union, with the instruction that the message be passed on to another, started what soon became a nation-wide link-up, advising the American worker which of the two candidates then on TV and rampage across the land was his friend and the man to give his vote. 'That's how we do it,' the spokesman sucked at his king-size cigar – which he was quick to point out that the father of Trade Unionism, Samuel Gompers, had himself patented. And to the query that the Chambers of Commerce, their directly opposite number in the American hierarchy, had charged the labour organization with having well over eight office blocks in the capital, when those with the millions made shift with one, the labour man, showing large and rather Dickensian features, had nothing but snorts and more puffs at his huge cigar. 'Gompers made the cigar,' he said. It was a statement as simple and symptomatic of the American scene as when earlier in the course of that second visit the Chambers of Commerce man had said in all seriousness: 'It is good for big business to organize but bad for labour to unite, because one is in the best tradition of free enterprise while the other is denying the individual his right to work.'

These sharp divisions and differences of interests do not however make the American worker a socialist, if they certainly consecrate the capitalist as a Conservative, with his Churchillian motto of 'What we have we hold.' On the contrary the only agitator America can well afford is the delinquent lone ranger fighting a losing war with society. In fact the belief seems to be that if you are smart you must surely reach the sky; the millions who happen not to have done so really have themselves to blame, and their rotten luck, not anybody else or government, or party. Those were more or less the defiant words thrown in my face by a girl friend. We had taken to each other at a warm house party in winter for a number of young people from the film industry. Many of them, it seemed, were out of a job. Indeed the joke there that night was that the party was to announce the fact that the host was out of a job again! That too happened to be the lot of the plump girl I came to date pretty often. A graduate of political science, she had nobody to blame but herself for being unemployed. I offered her a job there and then – that of typing me some manuscripts. And though she was full of thanks, offering to do a page for much less than I had been paying at Princeton, she laughed to scorn my idea of people expecting governments to do things for them. 'Why, that will be turning Jack into everybody's uncle, and already the family is so insufferable!'

And these are views well propped up from the other end of the ladder by those on top. On my second official trip to Washington in April, I fell talking in the train with a businessman of the Delaware Valley, a region reputed to be the most industrialized in all the US. He had a large construction business all built up from scratch by himself. And this he was going to make over to his son in the true tradition of all vast family fortunes. 'See him?' He whipped out of his breast pocket and notebook the photograph of a young man in military academy uniform.

'How are you sure he wants to follow in his father's footsteps?' I asked.

'He darned well will want to,' the man said. 'Why, he'll all be provided for. I have built this business up for what it is today so no member of my family will lack for anything.' And here he brought out another photograph, this time of the entire family, even with the old parents included. Radiant in the centre with a strapping son and two daughters on her either side was his wife.

'Now, they are all pretty well taken care of, for now and the future as far as human hand can provide.' He congratulated himself and the American system of which he was a shining 'success' example.

'Don't you think by all this provision and security, you deny them their great American privilege of paying their own way through life?' I asked.

'How is that?' he showed genuine surprise and disbelief.

'Well, I can appreciate the point of your doctors when they say they want no medicare for the old,' I began.

'Go on,' he prompted me, calling out for more drinks for us both in the bar where we sat.

'As I see it, the doctors seem to be insisting that every American citizen should have provided for himself fully by retirement age. So why ask government now to pay their full medical bills?'

'That's right, boy, you've been following pretty close our American debate,' he cheered me on. Until I added:

'Well, it seems to me you are denying exactly that sacred principle the doctors are insisting on by wanting to lay on everything for members of your family.'

'Young man, are you calling all my life's effort vain? No,

no, don't withdraw or make any apologies for beliefs you
honestly hold to. But tell me, as a writer, of what I don't
know, don't you want to make money?'

'Well, yes,' I hedged 'but the money side, although most
welcome, usually is secondary. The act of writing and the
creation that comes out of it are what matters.'

'Whew!' he whistled in mirth. 'You are a most interesting
young man. Look me up at George Town Inn, will you,
while you are in Washington,' he patted me on the shoulder.
And then turning to the barman, fired a parting shot: 'Let
the young man from Africa have as much beer as he wants.
Just send the bill to me – up in the first Pullman Coach.'

'Oh, thanks a lot,' I gripped his outstretched hand, rather
palpably hit, though not fatally, by his broadside that one had
to make money, and lots of it, to be able to meet bills, especially those run up by others.

Political parties in America, when we look at them with
regard to class, and distribution of wealth therefore tell
nothing. Rather they appear to the stranger two mutually
accommodating rival clubs into which members simply get
drawn by accident of birth or adoption. Each has little of the
ideological to persuade a convert as against the other; so
contradictory and self-cancelling are their so-called right and
liberal wings, and so absurd and mocking is the term Democrat for the rabid, conservative, racialist of the South who runs
the majority party of that name, it has even been suggested
by a number of wits that each party be sliced in two and the
equivalent halves of right and liberal fused to make new
wholes that at least will have some meaning and significance.
History itself alone knows how many times the terms Republican and Democrat have actually changed hands or merged
between both clubs. But every four years some fellow has to
be elected to the presidency to hand out largesse, and
naturally each club wants that honour for its member.

I did not see a filibuster in action in either House of
Congress, but the little I saw of the manoeuvring on the hill

was not a campaign calculated to win entirely my humble cheers. There were those House Committees, midwife to every bill dropped in the hopper or on the clerk's desk; but because each Committee had to be headed by its most senior member, the midwife often was dotty and possessed of the will and nerves to stifle any child not pleasing to her sight. Add to this the all-powerful Rules Committee, which can leave the new-born child to die outright or dwindle away in its incubator, the chances of a non-favourite bringing forth fruit appear very slim indeed.

But all this was sacrosanct to my Colonel and his ilk, and at no time would he allow my playing the iconoclast. Which was natural, except that he chose not to talk direct to me. Instead he asked Daniel Passent, my Polish colleague, and the one other fellow in the Parvin group who also persistently raised problems, although not with the same cheek as I, to plead with me that I was the embarrassment of everybody and had more than already proved the ruin of our outing and project. This mission I must say got home, for it left me for the rest of our stay in Washington prostrate with the twin feeling of amazement and amusement. Evidently, I did not quite get it out of my system, for on the fast train back to Princeton, after more giddy rounds of the city that left the most recourceful and disciplined time-server in the group dragging his feet, I found myself writing this epitaph from my general experience of Washington DC –

A morgue,
a museum –
Whose keepers
play at kings.

As a last act of homage and worship, we had also called at the White House just before taking off. President Kennedy was out at the back lawn receiving Italy's Premier Fanfani that morning, and we had the rare privilege of personally

being taken by Special Assistant to the President Ralph
Dungan through the executive mansion to watch host and
guest, a sharp study in height, review the guard of honour
mounted by the combined men of the US Armed Forces,
the mightiest the world has ever known. Of Jackie and
Caroline and John Junior we saw nothing; perhaps they were
upstairs in the balcony and nursery, watching the grand show
below. But we did see how much of the old colonial-type
mansion was already in the hands of the ultra-modern décor
people Jackie had herself called in. How it was all going to
end was an issue lying still in the bosom of the muses. One
object there, however, stood out prominent and definitive:
the Presidential Seal of the United States. Almost immediately and with a presence I found overwhelming, it drew
from me this final salute I captioned *Home from Hiroshima*:

> By decree
> Of the President of the United States
> Of America, unchallenged
> By factions on the hill,
> The eagle across the seal
> Has turned eyes
> Away from the arrows to the olive
> Shoot, so praise them who prospered most in war
> And now will live
> By peace. Yet in city
> And field, from coast to coast,
> The hail
> Of plumes, plucked, scattered free
> From the original breed,
> Shriek, thrash, rend the skies
> Till vengeance is
> Theirs, and likely
> At its own instance
> The wild west wreck the world.

9 · EJECTION!

A strange satellite was orbiting very low over the United States, so furiously low that millions of Americans milling from New York City to the village of Anaktuvule Pass in Alaska could see without the help of telescopes out in Cape Canaveral and California the burning body whirling above their heads. Looking very much like a huge helicopter ablaze with characters too weird to decipher by witch-catchers like the Central Intelligence Agency and Federal Bureau of Intelligence, the strange foreign body in the air, showering out sparks and streamers in the wake of its own storm, in a matter of one flash and swirl had left the entire sky over the sub-continent running and awash with a scarlet so terrible to the eyes that some called it blood and others fire.

Those old enough to remember thought it a thousand times more real and menacing than any hoax of a Martian raid Orson Welles had let loose, and on every lip was again that cry of disbelief and despair raised by all Americans when the first sputnik shot into space. Only now it carried the keen edge of the grave. Parents and children fought one another for safety of their shelter, pastors and executive directors shut out members of their flock and staff, schoolchildren milled into the streets before teachers could put lessons into practice, and the football game as well as baseball broke up in the bowl, with rattles, cans of beer and bags, capsules and canisters of lunch beating a scaring tattoo that an ever-on-the-alert militia and reserve corps could not answer. Only the scaremonger gangs of press and politicians kept well in character. What is Washington doing? they beat their breasts. Are the peace-loving people of America going to be strafed to death before the Administration does something? This sure is a Communist plot! Let's hop over and seize this here Cuba before Castro bombs us out! It's not just classified pictures of the US that that man Kruschev wants – why, look at that thing up above there! And you can be sure it carries H-bombs to blow up New York City, Washington DC, and Chicago! And what are we, the most powerful people on earth today, doing but standing around and listening to all that hogwash from the UN – a house fully occupied by black brats and commies?

On this occasion however the Administration was not waiting to be prodded; indeed it was already much ahead of the fastest running and fastest talking messenger of evil omen. Click, went the button to Omaha, whether from the President direct or from the Pentagon, always in alliance with Big Business, nobody it seemed might live to tell. But there for the cowards and the courageous to see with one catch of breath were squadrons of the Strategic Air Command long since air-borne and chasing the strange phenomenon for all their worth. It was like robins flying after an enchanter-owl. 'Will they catch up with him? Can they gun him down without harm to millions of Americans below?' The TV newscasters speculated soulfully. 'But first,' they broke off together 'shall we pause for a message – oh, yes, our sponsors have not for one moment lost faith in the will of the American people to overcome all their enemies.'

At this point exactly, sounds of sirens, as if all of New York

were already flooding with the blood or fire scarlet in the
skies, came with one crashing crescendo over the high and
low suds of the soap showing in the washing-machine, both
of which hordes of housewives, stuck and clinging to
their TV sets as a last resort, would very much want to
buy at the end of the invasion; and then the siren-sounds
drowned everything in that madhouse, on fire and out of
sight.

And I bobbed out also, from stream of sleep and dream on
the couch in my sitting-room and study, to hear the telephone
ringing away outside my door in the third entry of Princeton's
Graduate College. Someone, puffing down the steps, had
already picked the receiver up, calling out briefly: 'JP, it's
for you again!' I turned over on my side with one grunt after
another, for my temples were hammering as hard as if they
would split.

'Are you up?' Israel who had been my guest came up to
where I lay thrashing still half asleep.

'Ungh,' I grunted more.

'That call is for you,' he shook me.

'Ok, take it for me, will you?'

'Of course, yes.' I heard him run down the steps with the
fly-lightness of his figure, and then his quick, raucous voice
as he asked for who it was that wanted me that early Monday
morning.

'It's a Mrs Somebody,' he came back to tell me. 'Says she is
secretary to a Professor Patterson.'

'What does she want?' I shifted position to ease the pain
I felt in my every part.

'Don't know,' Israel said, 'but I can tell you she didn't hide
her Southern accent.'

'Hell.' I cursed aloud.

I scrambled out from under my wrapper, and staggered
out in my pyjamas into the stairway to take the call in person,
half a flight down.

'Hello,' I announced myself.

'Is that Mr Clark?'

'Yes.'

'When do you wake up?'

'Let's not go into that; now what is it you want?'

'I don't want anything of you; it is Professor Patterson, the Director of the Woodrow Wilson School, who wants you to see him.'

'Professor Patterson – the Director of the Woodrow Wilson School of Public and International Affairs?' I repeated after her.

'Yes, that's right.'

'When?'

'I cannot tell you. But are you free all today?'

'In the morning, yes.'

'Well, I'll find out from Professor Patterson when he can see you. He is at a meeting now.'

'And you have no idea what he wants me for?'

'No, Mr Clark, I have told you I do not know what the Professor wants to see you for. But I'll ring later and tell you the hour of appointment.'

'Thanks a lot.'

I hung up the receiver and stumbled up, straight back into bed. Israel had already finished his toilet, and closing the door behind him, looked at me with the anxious eye of the qualified doctor that he was, not of the quacks and powerful performers whose power and antics drove him out of the profession into the yet more sterile one of political study, but of a doctor still able to panic on behalf of a patient because he is a fellow creature in pain and needing personal help and care. I pulled my coverlet up over my face, and before he could find out what the matter was with me, the telephone bell went again and he ran out to take it.

'That woman again,' he returned immediately to report, 'and she wants you in person she says.'

So I pottered again, this time into deeper mystery and a growing sense of anger.

'Yes, Mr Clark, can you come over at nine tomorrow? Professor Patterson will be in the office to see you then.'

'So early?'

'Why, don't you have classes as early as that?'

'No, I don't.'

'Are you saying you cannot get up that early to attend classes?'

'Well, I happen not to have early classes.'

'You will have to come, anyway. The Director will be in his office between nine and eleven o'clock in the morning, and you'd better make sure you report there on time.'

'Well, about ten then.'

'What's that you say?'

'I said would ten-thirty to eleven suit the Professor?'

'Now you are calling the hour, but I'll find out from him and let you know. But try on your part, and call us.'

'Thank you.' After which I hugged the wall back into my room and bed. Israel, guessing that I wanted to rest more and be alone, lugged his bag of books to his shoulders and tramped out to the Firestone Library, a mile on the other side of the campus. I think I must have drowsed more with the dying of his footsteps down the steps and out on the walk through the inner court. When I woke up again with my body more relaxed and my senses beginning to focus, the smell of food was all about the place and I felt uncommonly hungry for breakfast, which I do not normally take. The hour bells of Princeton's many towers, always discordant and never agreeing among themselves, began then their staggered tolling, and looking at my watch, I saw it was long past noon. It now dawned upon me I had been up more than once before, and suddenly nightmare and the day's actual business each fell into place.

That terrible nightmare came actually as a repeat of my experience of America during the Cuban Crisis six months or more before. Then in Princeton the continuous tearing past overhead of jet-bombers and the horrid noise of other air-

craft taking off from military bases close by and returning
again from missions known only to those who had profits to
gain from plunging the world into war, would not let one
sleep. Nor would the mammoth parade by TV stations,
whether signing on or off, of all the armed forces and arma-
ment at the instant call and command of the American people
should that scoundrel Castro and his new-found uncle Nikita
Kruschev be mad enough to refuse moving out those
missiles aimed at the heart of the United States.

'Will you really go to war?' I had asked the Colonel who
I must add, grew almost youthful in those terrible days of
tension when every true American male expected to be called
up as if service like that would again save anybody.

'Yes.' He made no bones about the matter. 'The Russians
have played with us for too long. Now that we mean business,
we hope for their own good they take us seriously.'

'How are we for fall-out shelter?'

'Oh, very good,' the Colonel disclosed. 'The Firestone
Library can take the entire student body and faculty members
and their families, and quite a good number of town people to
boot.'

I thought of heavy walls crashing and damming up gates
to the underground shelter before the few left after the blast
had time to scurry like rats inside their holes, and of rubble
and tumbled down structures sealing up and burying people
alive like miners marooned in shafts and caves steaming hot
and perhaps flooding up as well. And then all in a flash I
recalled the stories and reports that a top-secret brain-
computing machine stationed on the campus actually dictated
to America's fleet of polaris and other nuclear submarines
where and when they must deploy themselves and fan-out
undersea in their long, deep dives to provide for America
and her Free World a constant invisible bulwark. In the event
of war therefore Princeton offered the Russians a palpable
hit, either directly or as part of the devastation that would
be New York or Philadelphia.

'Well, is that all the protection one can expect?' I laughed to cover up the cry in my throat.

'That's very good protection for anybody,' the Colonel said. 'There are millions not so provided for.' Which was true. Not that the millions thought much about the matter for themselves, anyway. There was the jolly fellow I shared drinks with at the Peacock Inn the night the Cuba quarantine was declared.

'What do you think of it all?' I asked.

'Me?' he spread out his arms. 'Kennedy is Irish and I am Irish. So what's there to say? Anything he does is good enough for me. I fought in Africa in the last War, and I guess am not too old to strap my boots on once more.' Such are the loyalties at work for the great American cause.

'And you have no plans to fly Parvin Fellows home?'

'No,' the Colonel ruled. 'They will have to take things as they come – with everybody, I'm afraid.'

'I think I better book myself a seat home on the next plane,' I said flippantly. And getting back into my room, I slept fitfully through that vision of America I had just dreamed a second time.

Odd, wasn't it? Recalling my imminent interview with the Director of the Woodrow Wilson School, an interview still carrying for me some air of mystery, I rang up his secretary to apologize for not calling much earlier and also to find out whether or not she had herself called as we seemed to have agreed and not got me. Professor Patterson's secretary was out for lunch, some neutral voice told me, but I could call again in an hour if I so wished. That suited me fine, for I could then have lunch myself. Because service in both the breakfast-room and Procter Hall was over already, and not having any stomach to fall across town for a meal, I made for the machine-room on the basement floor, and got myself some chocolate milk and cakes in real American fashion in praise of which I had written this little song:

A dime
  in the slot,
And anything
  from coke to coffee
Spews down your throat,
  from crackers to candy
Breaks against the enamel
  wear of your teeth,
(And as TV minstrels
  will have it ahead
Of the Congo
  and Guernica) tobacco
Enough to plant
  another Garden:
Now, old Moses
  for whom, they say,
Mannas fell in the desert,
  did he push a button as this,
  and who knows at what price?

Professor Patterson's secretary was back in her seat when I rang the Woodrow Wilson School later. I began with trying to say how sorry and ashamed I was that I overslept and failed to call her back earlier in the day to confirm the hour of appointment, but she seemed either too busy working to listen or was just not interested in long explanations and excuses.

'Mr Clark, you failed to call me back. Now, why didn't you? That's gross disrespect, the like of which has not been seen here before, a student telling the professor when he would be pleased to present himself for an interview. Anyway, Professor Patterson has now directed that you turn up unfailingly at nine tomorrow morning,' she spouted over me without stop.

'Excuse me,' I began.

'Now, Mr Clark, there is nothing to excuse. I think you fully understand all I have said.'

'Well, we shall see,' I said mysteriously and placed back the receiver on her, for she had started spouting again.

That was how things had been in the few days past. Returning from a brief trip up to Canada the week before, I had joined the rest of the Parvin group for our second pilgrimage to Washington. It had turned out a most tiresome affair. Arriving a little after eight in the evening by train, we had each been claimed and whisked off by host families, all prosperous sons of Princeton. I got billeted with my Nigerian colleague at the William Wrights, real estate people. They were most kind to us, although living out in Virginia, from where Mr Wright had to drive us into town every morning on his way to work, I half expected any moment to be called 'nigger' to my face, and given the necessary works therefrom. On the one occasion our host could not take us direct to where the long day's journey began for us into night, we hopped a bus into town. That seemed to send a shock of silence from aft to stern of the vehicle, accompanied by a spontaneous shying and shooing away movement and a shaking out of dress on the part of other riders, all of them whites, naturally. But that is another story entirely.

What did happen to me however was the merciless drill and systematic brainwashing that formed the Parvin lot ad nauseam all the session, but more blatantly in the course of those Washington pilgrimages. A two-hour visit to a '23 million jobs' school exhibition at the patio of the Department of Agriculture building, and briefings at the hands of AID programme officials lasting more than three hours in the State Department took up all the morning. Then 'individual interviews with appropriate State Department area officers' followed hot after a late lunch in the cafeteria there, a large classified affair. And taking the rest of the day was a visit to the Housing and Home Finance Agency, where a representative of Dr Weaver, who is a Negro conspicuously heading a full government department, told the silliest trash about housing and urban renewal feats, as if he did not know that everybody there knew what cheating and removal and uprooting of those already poor and blighted went under guise of that well-meaning operation called urban renewal.

We had a buffet supper that evening at the palatial home of the Hon. Mr and Mrs Andrew Berding, way out in the posh suburb of the capital. The Hon. Mr Berding had served in the Eisenhower administration as Assistant Secretary of State for Public Affairs, but now, more or less retired from public affairs, engaged himself completely with writing and lecturing. Very urbane and warm, he told us anecdotes late into the night which made my eyes flood with laughing. Although it was dark and we could not inspect the garden and admire its flowers and general layout, I passed a most pleasant and delightful time in the porch with Mrs Berding, talking flowers, how to breed new kinds, from the rose, red and white, to the hydrangea, dogwood, azalia and tulip, all beginning to blossom and shout out the arrival of spring, after a sharp, long winter, the severest within living memory. And as a grand finale underscoring the perfect union and bliss that was 'the Berdings', husband and wife played us their favourite pieces, one on a musical saw, the other accompanying on the piano.

'Oh, how beautifully you play together!' a female guest there gushed. 'Your timing is just great.'

'It ought to be; we've been at it for more than thirty years together,' Mrs Berding, eyes a bit glassy now, said briefly. I thought she was going to cry. Altogether theirs was a performance most charming and soothing. In fact, when a friend's wife drove in from somewhere in the city centre to collect me home at about midnight, it seemed churlish to tear myself away from a party showing no signs of breaking up for the night.

'He now moves with the millionaires,' my friend reported to her husband.

'Well, why didn't you tell them about us poor struggling

students and family from Nigeria? We need money, you know,' he said. 'One can't go on rushing from one job to another a whole day for much longer. It's giddy and maddening.'

'You are telling me,' I slumped into a seat. 'I have always wondered how you carry it off in addition to studying full time.' It had been a long slogging day, and another was already then hard on its heels.

That day, a Friday, began with a call at the head offices of the US Chamber of Commerce. There we heard from a smug spokesman of the Chamber a dreary lecture 'on the role of business in US political process and society', a talk with a most exasperating tone, marked by the man's straight-faced declaration that it was good for big business to organize but bad for workers to have trade unions which was denying the individual his right to find employment. Happily, his were claims soon offset by those put forward by the rough-hewed Dickensian character who addressed the Parvin group on the 'role of labour in the political process of the nation, the general outlook on technological change, automation and retraining of displaced workers'. It was a fine contrast in the debating styles of two formidable proponents of the American way of life which, both were equally emphatic in stating, secured its firm foundation on the rock of private property and ownership arising from free enterprise that no Communist or Socialist lever could displace or topple over with talks about ownership of means of production and a fairer distribution of national wealth.

Break for lunch came like a fresh burst of air into the stuffy room each spokesman for America was bent on making the place for me. It was more so as Mimi and Eldon Crowell had come over and collected Dan Passent and me to have lunch with them at Washington's club for top lawyers, of which Eldon was a member. For us two Parvins, that really was a break-through of sun and sunshine in a sky oppressive with clouds.

In the afternoon, piloted by a gentleman from the Foreign
Student Service Council, the group, striving very much to
remain together, toured the American Indian Hall at the
Smithsonian Institution of Natural History, and went desul-
torily on from there to the National Archives. It was here
that I realized for the first time that Lincoln's famous
emancipation proclamation actually was directed solely at and
effective only in the Union-occupied South, so that for a
chaotic interval during which self-righteous Northern States
searched their hearts and factories and farms, white masters
and black slaves did not know for sure on what side of the
line they stood. Washington, much steamier than Lagos, was
teeming that Friday with wide-eyed, young and old pilgrims
visiting from distant states the shrines of George Washington and Abraham Lincoln. And moving among these crowds
looking so lost among the relics and replicas of their ghost
past, and having my grey retired public-servant pilot close by
my side, since all others had either deserted or simply passed
out, I felt rather like Dante being shown by Virgil through
the various regions of punishment and pleasure in the
underworld.

This then provided the backdrop against which the petty
drama of my last days at Princeton, and indeed in the United
States, was enacted to the exclusion of an outside audience
and body of independent adjudgers and critics.

I did not turn up at nine on Tuesday morning at the offices
of the Director of Princeton University's Woodrow Wilson
School of Public and International Affairs. Later in the day,
someone, I think it was that overbearing secretary again,
called to say I had a most urgent and important letter to
collect from my pigeon-hole at the School. I was not around
but went over immediately to take delivery as soon as I was
told of it. 'Dear Mr Clark,' it directed without much ado,
'Will you please arrange with Mrs Sangston a meeting with
me on Wednesday, April 24, to discuss the question of
whether your fellowship should be continued beyond May 1.'

And appended at the bottom was the personal seal and signature of Professor Patterson, the Director.

My first reactions prompted that I simply ignore the note, for what it was worth. I was due to go down with the rest of the Parvin crowd at the latest on May 13. Indeed, Colonel Van de Velde, our ubiquitous stage manager and more, already appeared genuinely to be losing sleep and weight over the failure of some of us to submit to him the plan and itinerary for our individual round-country tour of the United States in fulfilment of the last part of the Parvin bargain before going our different ways home.

I rather looked forward to that advisory session with the Colonel. When I went to Cornell University at Ithaca in Northern New York State and to Canada across the border, he had proved most useful, not only in making funds available, but especially in the plotting out of routes. There, with a map spread out over the litter on his desk, he charted out for me on each occasion the course of my trip, down to the last detail of execution. Old soldiers never die, I said silently to myself in honest admiration. And in my mind's eye I tried to picture the man just as he must have looked in camp, as well as on the field in occupied France. All this was a scene I looked forward very much to seeing him re-live in however obscure an operation.

Meanwhile, I thought I should first make sure of my booking on a boat sailing for the Far East and India from San Francisco on the West Coast on June 23. Confirmation came at last from the Cunard Shipping Line in New York. So I began working out where and what I would like to see more of the United States. The deep South for me was a top issue. I said that would be the first place I would go if I was going to tour the country at all. The Colonel however would not hear of it, offering a stout and sincere resistance which won my praise and thanks not a little. A Rhodesian Parvin had gone South in the last year in company of two white friends, and for all the segregation and discrimination he had suffered before at home, he came back a deeply hurt man, having in addition helped to spoil a pleasant holiday for his friends. Now, that fellow, though a journalist like me, was a most charming and accommodating guy. I got the tip all right.

'I still want to go down South and see things for myself,' I insisted.

'Well, you brought some native costumes with you, didn't you?' The Colonel sought a new line of action.

'And what may those be?' I asked.

'Don't get me wrong,' he said wanly. 'All I mean is whether you have your Nigerian dress with you.'

'Like which?' I teased him.

'Well, I had in mind those colourful flowing robes – now, what do you call them? Africans around here and in New York and Washington wear them pretty often.'

'You mean the agbada and sokoto?'

'Say that again,' he urged, removing his leg off the arm of his chair. 'Yes, I think, if you insist on going South, now those are the things you should wear all the time. With your tribal marks showing in addition, they ought to convince everybody you are no American Negro.'

'I don't have any such clothes, not even at home in Nigeria,' I explained.

'Really?' the Colonel expressed surprise.

'Honestly,' I assured him. 'We have lots of dresses in Nigeria, depending on where you come from, although the Yoruba agbada has fast become the adopted style with many, especially the Easterners. I know of friends in the Foreign Service who have worn European dress all their lives, but on getting posted abroad, ran off to the market to have that kind of Nigerian dress prominent in their wardrobes.'

'Isn't that what they call projecting the African Personality?' the Colonel asked humorously. 'That's the first thing I thought you would do coming over here. Your friend from Nigeria is simply delightful in his gorgeous costumes. At parties he makes quite a splash in them.'

'Yes,' I agreed. 'He adopted them back home.'

'Aren't you a strange one? A nationalist and fighter like you, without your national costume! I think you ought to borrow some from your friend before thinking of going South.'

'Not to carry out a masquerade,' I frowned. 'If I cannot go anywhere I want to in this country without fear of harm or harassment, then I don't see where all your talk about freedom and equality leads us.'

'Well, I confess it is a great shame things are like this in the US. Still, we are trying. I'm only trying to be honest with you. There's no point in having you run off South with your temper as it is. You will only get hurt badly, and then we shall be called to give account. You ought to go to the New England States, or go to the Mid-West and see the Grand Canyon, the Salt Desert and national parks out in the North-West – they are all splendid sights. And of course you must go to California, the climate is just like yours, only with the steam off. Now this is the tour I should be planning had I the good fortune to be in your shoes.'

That was the last friendly talk I had with the Director of the Parvin Programme at Princeton, and it came before our journey of torment to Washington. After that, like an incensed manipulator of lights in the theatre, he began switching all the lights off around me on the stage, just when I was preparing to take the cue for the formal finishing act, and then make a quiet if not graceful bow-out.

I called on Professor Patterson at his offices at eleven on Wednesday morning. Mrs Sangston, his secretary, gave me to understand that the Director was at that moment engaged with one or two other professors, and in the meantime would I please take a seat and wait my turn. After some ten minutes, Professor Patterson came out with his visitors, bade them good morning, and then turning my way, waved me into his office.

I recognized him immediately as the gentleman who had laughed quite a lot and very easily at a small house party Professor Livermore and his wife had held for us Parvin Fellows in the home of two lady friends of his right at the beginning of session. I had not met him since, as he too pointed out, as he explained the nature of the painful duty others had advised him to perform by me that morning. Hands in his pockets, when he was not blowing his nose (the effect of a slight cold, he apologized) the Professor, quite small, especially for an American, paced in the small space between his chair and the wall behind, looking out every now and again through the window at the street immediately outside and the John Foster Dulles Annexe to the Firestone Library showing just beyond. It seemed to take him some time coming to the point. I tried in that interval to explain on my side why there had been the apparent wrangling over fixing this appointment. The trouble was that I allowed myself to be drawn into a quarrel with a secretary who I thought was most rude.

'Oh, that's all right,' the Professor dismissed that episode. 'She has been doing that job for almost thirty years, and nobody has found her wanting before. But to come to the subject of our meeting this morning,' he stayed my protest, 'you got my letter, I hope.'

'Oh, yes,' I said. 'I am rather puzzled by it. The programme is over except for the round-trip portion of it. So I don't see how the need arises for an extension of my fellowship. Are those for the others under review as well?'

'Well, that's the problem,' the Professor stated. 'The programme this year is as you say all but ended, and everybody preparing for his journey to wherever he pleases in the US before returning to his own country and job. Now the question is, Mr Clark, whether you have personally gained anything from coming here to Princeton and the United States as a whole.'

'I don't follow what you mean.'

'Let's put it this way then,' the Professor sat back in his seat. 'I hear from the Director of the Parvin Programme that you have not been attending classes, and others in the group have been making full use of courses available here at Princeton.'

'I have sat in the classes I thought useful.'

'And which are these?'

'I took a course in International Politics –'

'That was the first term, and Professor Sprout reports that you dropped out in the last weeks.'

I recalled those classes in International Politics, a discipline not so new now but still doing all in its power to appear logical and scientific, vying in that process with all the natural sciences, especially physics, including nuclear physics at that, in finding a formula for every action of a politician who happened to be prime minister or president, as if politicians even more so than other human beings acted according to fixed patterns of behaviour that the pet theories of professors could track down. Professor Sprout, always in a spruce suit and behind dark glasses, was something of a pioneer in the field. As a matter of fact, he and his wife had brought out at that time a new compendious volume on the subject, a work that modesty never quite allowed him to include in the fat reading list he drew up for members of the class. These consisted mainly of serious-minded young men undergoing this rigorous training in preparation for their teaching assignments later in life. But others were men who had already seen action in the public service of the United States, ranging from a rather panicky and talkative diplomat, who had served in Cuba and other missions in Latin America, to a stocky, solid, silent vice-admiral or officer not much farther down the ladder. 'Do you think Krushchev can defend Castro all the way from Moscow?' I had said to him during the Cuba debâcle.

'Well, I am not at all happy and sure about our own logistics,' he had told me.

It was in this class I had first met Israel Rosenfield, a brilliant MD now turned candidate for the PhD in politics. Nobody could understand such a change. On the other hand, with his scientific training and a mind exceptionally sharp, he seemed to understand all pretensions and professions there gathered, and because he could not keep to himself the diagnosis for which he personally very much wanted a cure, he got into no end of trouble. 'Oh, that young man,' the Colonel on our way from Ford's Mahwah had admitted hearing of him, 'he fights every problem. Quite like you!' And there were several things needing proof from life, as day in day out in the large classroom down on the basement floor at the Woodrow Wilson Building, one saw the world chopped up and quartered into two polar camps, one the free world, the other the Communist bloc, each lurking like savages or beasts of prey in the dark to eat up the other unto the last. Boxes, circles, arrows, or genealogical trees formed the favourite and familiar symbols and audio-visual devices and aids endlessly chalked up on the blackboard to catalogue and analyse national ideologies, international groupings and alliances, and the emergence and direction of new blocs on the world scene, stressing how ineffective these were without a striking nuclear stockpile like that possessed by the Americans and the Russians. One camp, it seemed, had more of a dynamic philosophy to live by vis-a-vis the worn-out Christian beliefs peddled by the other. But these were sentiments and surmises quickly wiped off the board. 'One never knows if the FBI chaps are around,' the professor used to warn them as he made sure of a clean slate on the wall.

One pet subject of those classes was that of the famous Games Theory. Put in crude layman terms, it goes like this. Suppose two roads were open to two opposing groups of soldiers, and one camp had to use one of these roads at all costs. Which should its commanding officer choose since the enemy has both under strict watch? Either way, and by a toss-up, says the game theorist! In other words, a complete abandonment of a calculated and reasoned-out choice, and reliance in a blind plunge, since the enemy knows already anyway all the plans possible. Haphazard as it may sound to the simple ear, the top strategists and policy-makers of the great powers seem to have taken for quite some time now many a decisive move, fraught with dangers for millions, by simply playing this game, so like a blind-man's buff to the novitiate. And the absolute virtue of the top-secret, super-guarded computer on the campus, I was told, lay in its powers to dictate the hazard at the peril of the enemy. For example, the perpetual stationing of America's nuclear striking submarines deep in the Atlantic and elsewhere. Or to cite a more down-to-earth, work-a-day instance. How should America react if it came to the hearing of the President and the public that one US citizen was bumped off in Moscow? Now, the expected and safe answer can always be got by a diligent application of the master mind to the game – to satisfy conditions varying from a street brawl to the planting of missiles in a sphere belonging to another; or so the lectures suggested.

'Dr Van de Velde himself expressed surprise that I stuck it that long, almost to end of term,' I offered an excuse. 'The whole course had little to do with events happening in actual life. And as a journalist that's all I deal with.'

'That may be so,' Professor Patterson conceded. 'But could you tell me what other things you have done since coming here and which you have found of benefit?'

'Well, I have been attending a course on the Development of American Literature –' I began.

'Professor Thorpe says he has not seen you for some time,' he cut in quietly.

'I have been absent for a couple of times,' I defended myself like the real schoolboy and truant they had made me out to be. 'Yes, I missed classes only two or three times, and on those occasions I had good reasons to – in fact the professor himself permitted me, for example, when I was going to give a reading at Adelphi College.' Incidentally, that was a performance I heard later was broadcast by the Voice of America and beamed all over Africa, without their first seeking my permission or making any payment since.

'Well, apart from the Parvin seminar compulsory for the group but which I hear you missed going to quite a number of times, you cannot really pin down any particular course you have done. The professor who takes the Comparative Politics course for which you registered says he doesn't even remember your face. It is evident therefore Princeton has had nothing to offer you.'

At that stage of the interview, I thought I might as well have a really straight talk about it, since it became then pretty obvious that the Colonel had taken great care and pains to compile his case. I reviewed for the benefit of the professor the attempts the Colonel and I had made together to find me a suitable course to pursue at Princeton for that one year and special programme I was there. In the Politics Department we had found no opening of practical value, nor had Professor Downer's English School, except for Professor Thorpe's classes held later in the session and several miles out in his home on the outskirts of Princeton. Philosophy, psychology, economics, architecture, and all the other fields of study like engineering and the physical sciences, for which the place is justly famous, I had shown no nose or training for. So at one point it was suggested that I should go and attend undergraduate classes on creative something or the other.

'Professor Patterson, had I come for a second degree,' I began, 'I should know what to do and how to set about it. A Parvin Fellowship is hardly the way to that.'

'That's right.' The professor punctuated me.

'Well, I wouldn't try to dispute the charge about those courses, except perhaps to state that even if I regarded myself as a regular student, that should not remove my right to skip classes and pay for it at exams.'

'That's the British system, isn't it?'

'But I wouldn't say I have wasted my time coming here,' I tried to assure him.

'How have you used it?'

'Well, beside attending those classes they are good enough to concede me, I have done a couple of plays and written a number of poems since coming here.'

'Couldn't you have done that elsewhere other than coming here?'

'Yes, one of the plays, perhaps, but not the poems which mostly are out of my US experience.'

'So you could easily have locked yourself up in a New York hotel and done the same thing. We have not given you a sabbatical, have we?' he asked. There was a sudden twinkle to his eyes.

'Well, I suppose that's a legitimate charge, but I should have thought the Parvin fellowship was to allow me room for development here in Princeton.'

'That may be so, but the fact is that you have shown disdain for everything Princetonian and American. That has been the impression of everybody here who has expressed an opinion about you.'

'Disdain how?'

'You see, we don't mind people talking politics and socialism here. That's not the point at all. This is a healthy community. You may not find all that you want here. Your colleagues however, seem to have, as have thousands of others. So do you think it is of benefit to you and us that your fellowship continues?'

'Is there anything left of it but the round-trip?'

'That's exactly the point,' the professor underlined it for me to see. 'You have spent much of your time out of here travelling while others stayed in and studied. Now it is their turn to go out.'

'That's fair enough.'

'Well, what do you think we should do with you?'

'What does a guest do when the host shows him the setting sun?'

'Well, we don't want any bad feelings, but it is the opinion of all that, since you have shown nothing but disdain for Princeton and the US, there could be no point in continuing the association further.'

'Thank you,' I said, rising to go which brought the professor also to his feet, hands in his pockets again. 'And how soon am I expected to leave here?' I asked.

'That would be for Dr Van de Velde to work out. But I suppose as soon as he can straighten out things with the Graduate School people.'

'One point I should like cleared. Does this end here in Princeton? I mean, can I continue with any activities I have outside of here?'

'The point, well, is this. Once your association with Princeton terminates, the College, I think, will write accordingly to the Immigration Authorities to state they are no longer sponsoring you for the visa you may be holding, and in that case, I gather, there is nothing left for you but to leave the US immediately. But I should ask Dr Van de Velde about that.'

'I see.' I said goodbye.

The Colonel had the administrative details of my departure already well in hand, when I brushed past his breathless secretary, who, it goes without saying, knew everything. Surprisingly, and even beyond my own expectation and the promise I had given the other Parvin people, who at this point wanted to take all sorts of steps impossible for their kind, I appeared most collected and calm for my last interview with the old Colonel. This seemed to unsettle him, for he literally jumped at me when, taking the liberties of a valedictory speech, I expressed surprise and a sense of injustice that the private and recruit had not been warned earlier in the campaign of his shortcomings. That would have offered the rascal a fair chance of either choosing to fall into line or quitting at the outset. Instead the company commander, showing no real sign of offence or concern at any time, had left him unreprimanded, only to have him courtmartialled at the point of general and final discharge, booting him out in ignominy at the last minute.

'Don't you teach me how to do my duties, you whipper-snapper!' the Colonel lunged dangerously at me. I could see from the corner of my eye his secretary start out of her seat. 'I'll throw you out of here now on your neck if you try any more of your cheek here.'

'Well, you certainly have thrown me out on a limb already,' I said sweetly.

'You have been a delinquent student, a disgrace to the College and your country. You were brought here as a journalist and an ambassador, but what have you done with all the opportunities placed at your disposal here?'

Still maintaining a sweetness and calm foreign to me, I asked whether the occasional absence from classes made one a delinquent student, especially where grades were not taken and no examinations were sat for to tell the best parrot. I also made it clear that at no time did I regard myself as rep-resenting anybody or any country, and therefore whatever disgraceful acts I had done must be visited on me alone as a free and willing agent of myself alone.

'Well, we have law and order here, and let me tell you, young man, I have seen more life and been to better places than you. We must have law and order; society cannot afford to go on with persons like you.'

'Any society should be able to afford a maverick,' I said softly.

'No, that will corrupt other citizens who are regular in their conduct,' ruled the Colonel.

'Isn't it because they are so regular that you get the mavericks?' I asked slyly.

'Now, don't try your cleverness on me. I can't argue with you.' The Colonel drew the line.

Later, with him reclined and rocking every now and again in his chair, having first wiped off the specks of foam that had sprouted about the corners of his mouth, the Colonel listened soberly to my complaints about the abruptness of my leaving, why on earth this had happened to me at that point of my life, and what it was I was then supposed to be going back to when I left Princeton in disgrace and such haste.

'You have your newspaper job to go back to, haven't you?' the Colonel reflected.

'No, I resigned that, I told you, before coming over here.'

'Of course, you can always pick up a job when you return home,' he stood firm.

'Well, that's one of the mis-assumptions by people, especially of our programme; that once you have come over for some course of study or in-service training, then you become overnight an expert for every problem in your under-developed country. Unless you were already in the top positions that matter, like our own General from Somalia, for example, you cannot jump the junior post you were serving in to go and direct others because you have been at Princeton, and personally, I don't see any job I can go into now without a whole board sitting over it first. You'll agree these things take time.'

'Well, you are a poet and playwright, aren't you?' he said with a mischievous cutting edge he could not succeed in containing inside its sheath.

'Now it's you saying so,' I laughed.

The following day, in the midst of my packing and awkward explanations to curious colleagues at the Graduate College, I received this letter from the Colonel, written in his own masculine hand. It minced no words. 'Mr Clark, you

will receive, within the next few days, $100 (stipend for
May) plus $25 (help for sending your heavy luggage home)
plus $100 (for expenses incidental to your travel home). A
total of $225.

'Whenever your heavy (sea) baggage is ready, let Mrs
Krulisch know and she will call the freight forwarder
Harbourt, so he can make arrangements with you –

R. W. V.'

'Well, there goes your $700 travelling money, and all
because you won't shut your bloody trap,' someone said,
handing the ejection note round the small group of friends not
quite decided among themselves whether I should be pressed
on to stay or be seen take off immediately as I already
proposed to do.

'It's so mean of them.'

'I told you Princeton is a lousy place.'

'The Parvin Fellows ought to rise as a body and threaten
them with going off with JP if they don't behave more
sensibly.'

'There you are asking too much – $700 is no small
money to forego.'

'Mr Parvin himself I hear is coming from California to a
farewell party of theirs next week. Now, that's the man to
tell how they are administering the programme he finances.'

'Perhaps the Graduate College should do something
before then.'

'This treatment of JP, rude as he is, is a negation of all
that programme stands for.'

All this, so genuinely sympathetic and indignant, was
highly interesting and explosive stuff to come from my close
circle of student friends, many of them Americans. But to have
hoped that they or the Parvin Fellows would rise to a man
and upturn by force or persuasion what the Princeton
authorities had already decreed would have been like expecting America's six million unemployeds and bums, not
mentioning the twenty million Negro people burdened by

their colour and history, actually forming a large portion of these 'superfluous people', as a TV commentator called those of the lower depths of America, to march in their tattered and starved hordes and columns upon Wall Street or Capitol Hill.

For that would be revolution indeed, and revolution of any type for the American is a state and ideal already completely and permanently achieved at home by their founding and fighting fathers several centuries back; and today, it is an objective the Central Intelligence Agency may carry out in dictator-ridden Latin-American republics and Socialist-minded Afro-Asian developing states on behalf of Big Business, the powerful lobby with its hand on the steering-wheel of the diplomacy and foreign policy in Washington. The rub however, as its former Chief Allen Dulles put it with great bite and aplomb before a very amused Princeton audience, could well be that the Central Intelligence Agency might be effecting a coup in some Middle East country while the head of it is being entertained in Washington as an honoured guest by the President and Congress!

In a set-up like that, it is no wonder the American student is so well-contained and content inside his coarse tights and emblazoned jerseys. To pile up grades, he chews hard at studies just as he does at his sweet gums and ice-cream. Games at their best are the pre-occupation of the giant breed, cheered on equally by special athletics scholarships and a colourful thumping college brass band and chorus of acrobatic co-eds. On week-ends he will drive as far as the next state or beyond to reach his date who he may take out to the cinema, fondle and kiss good night at the parental or girl dormitory gates. But he may not slip out of that habit into the sloppy one of wanting to go to bed with her when they are not decently engaged and married. And the horror was great, if as happened often, the foreign students from Africa or even Europe expressed disappointment back in the hall of residence at the lack of accessibility of the American College girl who

is so coy and sex-scared. Only at Princeton's highly hierar-
chied set-up, falling into ranks of colour, wealth, education,
and age, you could never quite tell whether your American
colleague was horrified at your desires because you happened
to be of another colour or country!

At Princeton's Graduate College, for example, students, I
found, were more or less satisfied, indeed were excited to
the point of actually shouting yodels, by the mere presence in
their midst of guests coming in from girls' colleges like Bryn
Mawr. 'Mixers' they call such meetings. Procter Hall often
provided the setting for the idyllic picture of innocent mating
and coupling. There with tall candles lit on brass stands on
the breavy boards, boys and girls would sit and dine late of a
Saturday night, sipping sherry and swapping know-how on
the latest gadgets, car models, and smart ideas in astronomy
or sociology. Those flickering candles, a wit once said
unkindly, were to ensure that hosts did not see their guests
too close in the face, for these often were most plain if not
straight ugly!

Incidentally, woman-lover as I am, I too could not help
noticing the determined manner most American girls,
especially the college ones, set about making themselves look
unattractive and in fact much like the males who, paradoxically,
are a most good-looking people. But the American young
female, in her court shoes and knee-high hose, when she is in
a brief skirt and shorts and not in those ill-mended, rough-
and-tumble tights, and with hair down or bobbed over a face,
often chubby and irregular in feature, with perhaps a nose
too stubby or veering to the crinkly or crooked, provided for
me a constant object for sobering reflection far away from the
over-painted synthetic models on parade on celluloid. My
shock of discovery perhaps was equalled only by that
expressed by a New York tube-rider during the newspaper
black-out. There was then no wide double sheet for anybody
to cover their face. My, the tube-rider had told *Newsweek*, who
would have guessed New Yorkers were so ugly! I did not

venture to go that far, except to express my silent gnawing
hunger because –

> The mannequins
>   in the windows,
> Sure sirens
>   calling without
> Discrimination
>   down the streets,
> Do not make up for me
>   the Marilyn Monroes
> I miss among the smart coffee

Strange indeed that that extraordinary creation and destruc-
tion by Hollywood, long gone beyond the pale of death as they
put it, but who in life was even farther away from my kind
behind a more damning barrier of colour, and perhaps,
celebrity, should have formed for me the heart of that hunger
for beauty and love, shouted everywhere by America but
which she really cannot satisfy. I made a humble wreath to
her name that I strung out like this:

> Wellbeing is a bed
> Of rubber foam that
> Possessed, rocks as
> Asleep. And not just
> The body, but spirits
> Sink with sirens. Pain
> Is the pin or thorn,
> That a foundling around,
> Stabs us to waking. Which is
> Hard to endure. Thus
> Hands softer than
> Down, fairer than
> Flower, held both to heart,
> And flaked all with ash.

At Cornell University, however, where boys and girls compete on equal terms on the same campus, I once walked into a scene in one of the women's halls of residence, just at that time of signing in before lights are out, that I found most affectionate and touching. There in the gloaming of the hall, on a windy, snow-clad night, each boy returning to the larger world open outside the gates was an Orpheus, and each girl being commandeered away by the hall-warden was an Eurydice! After that, I did not exactly mind my own date repeating her mother's lesson to me that New York was not Ithaca, and it would therefore be difficult to continue our mixed dating there.

Grades, dates, and games therefore form the healthy pre-occupation of the American student. Protests and demonstrations are adolescent manifestations to be expected among the growing student bodies in the emergent and unstable societies of Africa, Asia, and South America. It matters very little that the Debating Union at Oxford or Cambridge and lately the campaign for Nuclear Disarmament spawns in Britain products that go direct to Westminster. American society, so fluid, they say, in many things, is however too set for that. In fact, for students to engage together in such pastimes in the United States would be to expose themselves to the charge of engaging in un-America activities. The fault therefore lies in their set-up, not in themselves for being dumb and un-demonstrative about events outside. Their one failing per-haps may be ignorance of trends and events happening abroad but which the press, TV and radio guardians do not think fit and proper to project and register on their conscious.

There was that controversy we had at Princeton over what foreign papers the Graduate College should retain in its common-room. Many of us from abroad voted for a continuation of our subscription to *The Times* of London, our argument being that not even the *New York Times* in all its amplitude quite carried all the important news items those of us from Latin-America, Europe, Asia, and Africa were pretty certain of reading a day after in the air-freighted edition of *The Times* of London. I took a bet with the Colonel, by the way, that story by story, and not just by linage, his bible *The New York Times* was nowhere near the ambling matron of the British Press in the coverage of foreign news. Neither of us won the wager as we never got down to the brass tacks of taking a comparative count. The row at the Graduate College raged on for days, and notice-boards got plastered several times over with disputatious personal letters and committee notes in wild approval or protest against retaining the services of Aunt Fleet Street. Symptomatic of all was one rebuff roundly delivered by an irate American graduate student: 'What do you want to read that red paper for? You must all be Commies!' But wrong labels and false accusations like this all really go back to the great ignorance and self-absorption of Americans as a prosperous self-sufficient people long safe behind the Atlantic and the Pacific and the walls of protective beliefs, tariffs and slogans they have raised about their freely acquired property.

Bars of sororities and fraternities, behind which American students safely operate, when not rioting and derailing trains to no purpose except that the sap of spring runs wild in their blue veins, as at Princeton, are not raised for aliens and the uninitiated; nor did I go out of my way to seek an opening and passage. But Professor Tumins of Princeton's Sociology Department once told us a story at the Parvin Seminar that could well be indicative of the attitude of mind of the typical member of these closed shops and clubs that the American student has made a special preserve. Apparently, there arose a diplomatic and political need among Princeton's exclusive student eating-clubs to have some black faces in their midst. This started a lot of arguing within the cabals and cliques. For which of the African students, in the absence of American Negro youths, were they to invite? Few as they were, they certainly could not all be invited. So a quota system, very traditional with the place, had to be worked out among the various clubs. And what criteria did they agree to apply to their African guests? First of these was that they must show a decent sense of dress – when the hosts themselves are so scruffily turned out! After that, I did not care to hear out the rest of the list.

In my last week of scuttling from Princeton with a few feckless hands trying hard to effect a salvage of some sort, there were inevitably precious possessions and objects I tried very hard to clutch at and rescue, possessions and objects that proved most disconcertingly scarce to recollect in that period of crisis. Surprisingly, the one thing I missed in the US and which I still regret very much was the break-up of my ties with a couple of Negroes out in their comfortable ghettoes and lone posts. I visited my folks of St John's Street, as I came to call them, quite frequently for a time.

The man had been a Captain in the Army during the War but now he was quite contented with being an attendant by day in some Women's Club in Princeton. His wife worked at night as companion and watch for an old invalid widow or spinster with a lot of money. Together they made a jolly, bustling couple with their jobs, home, and children, the first of which had long since begun earning his own keep. The man used to say to me: 'Look at your friend who went to College, and to Princeton at that, how much dollar do you think he makes in a week with all his education? Of course, I regret not going to college or continuing with my commission, but look here, my wife and I here comb up quite a bit between us. Which is more than you can say for some people with all their libraries and airs.'

It was hard arguing this when examples abounded everywhere, depicting the ugly and unbelievable phenomenon in the American firmament of opportunity and plenty which makes many a cleaner and porter, with his odd shifts and spare-time jobs (called moonlighting), as well off as, if not better than graduate teachers and trained technicians. So although college, they say, is America's best friend, why shouldn't there be drop-outs, and at a very heavy rate too among the Negroes, when the unskilled and uneducated can perfectly well afford to marry the girls of their dreams, and both spouses can settle happily ever after in the regular home plus the automobile that are their combined dreams? The only snag is that the unskilled man might perhaps be more exposed to the dangers of settling down in a rut or getting rattled about in shallow grooves, whereas his compatriots with developed brains and skills may make a better fight of it, against automation, perhaps, and so move up the social scale with a fair degree of acceleration. Yes, this probably was so, agreed my St John's folks, and it certainly has been one of the cruel factors that have kept the black man down and out in America for so long. 'But things will sure change,' they cheered themselves. 'Why, look at you here drinking with us when President Goheen wants you over at the college to dine with him.'

My other couple, much older and more by themselves, have a thirteen-acre home on a hill some miles outside of Princeton. From there on a clear-skied day the visitor can see New Brunswick some twenty-five miles away. Not having children of their own, and constantly harassed now by land speculators and city planners making designs on their estate, my friends have turned their property into a trust. It was their hope when their large swimming pool was complete, to license the place as a community and holiday centre for the Negroes, just as the Jews and others do for their people. To this end, they actually invited me and other Parvins, that is, the coloured ones only, to dinner one night, so that each of us in turn, being so highly spoken of in Princeton, could bring over to the opening of the centre envoys and other influential people from our countries. Only their presence and sponsorship, they said, could convince the blacks of Princeton that it was time they all got together. Corporate action, the secret of big business corporations like RCA, all very vulnerable if only the black people of the earth will boycott them for exploiting them,

was what a centre like theirs would strive to foster in the
heart of members. And could all of us there help?

It was a pity they seemed not to know of the wary habits
of diplomats, Africans not excepted. And it was so painful
that I never saw them again before being chucked out of the
country of their birth and beleaguerment. It seemed a simple
and straight natural relation could not exist for long between
my American Negro friends and myself without their wanting
me to do something or another to help them. And not really
being in a position to help myself, I found it a better policy
keeping away, although this too was an unnatural and
impossible position. In such circumstances, I often found it
more congenial and convenient, while in New York, to walk
on Harlem's 125th Street, to skirt Times Square, and to
meander among the alleys of Greenwich Village, where for all
their pimps, prostitutes, dope-peddlers, and promiscuous
clients in homosexual pubs, you knew what exactly you were
being solicited for, what the risks and price were, and what
was more, your own capability, leaving no tender feelings of
loyalty and other susceptibilities trampled behind.

But moving to neutral, commercial ground and refusing to
get engaged and involved in the affairs of my embattled
friends only served to isolate me more, making me most
lonely when in the thick of that human mart where Broadway
becomes Times Square. After one such fruitless night of
seeking for lasting warm contact, I gave while waiting for my
bus connection at the Ports Authority Bus Terminal, the
following wail and yawn like a lost dog baying the moon –

> Day fell here:
> Like a drift of dead leaves,
> Day fell facewise among the blocks,
> And suddenly! down the overgrown plots,
> The great tall figures, all sterile
> And faceless before, are in woods
> Of a festal night conifer-like trees

Ablossom with fruit. All
Who earlier in the fall
Milled here to pluck or pick at a price
The apple or peach, have forced
Thro' the harvest, bitten by
Bugs, have followed nuts
Home to rabbit-holes,
To nest up among boles.
How stripped of sensations now the stalls
All stand – even like a strip-teaser
Without breast or hair!
    Two figures,
Fugitive from light, go kicking
Their shadows down steps belching up
The corner. Just then, as if in affectionate
Recognition, a wake of wrappings,
Fingers have fondled, tongues
Have sucked to stumps, blow
Them kisses with the gum-wetness
Of a wind limping also to bed.
    And I am
As the bum washed up on
The street, where markets are full
To fiesta, lesser by far than the scarecrow
Left over a farm, long after
Elephant trumpet and
      chorus of locust.

So acute grew the emptiness in me during my last days of shunting between Princeton and New York, while there appeared a flooding everywhere, that the final offerings Princeton had for my kind even swept me back to that place. It was like a dog returning to its place of vomit, more so as I had no stomach really for the fare. This was a fourfold feeling. First there was a farewell dinner given to the Colonel and other close faculty members by the Parvin Fellows, minus the

Yugoslavian, who refused to do anything which would deplete his funds any more. The one thing I recall of it is Barbara, the Colonel's wife, trying frantically to draw my attention to the fact without actually telling me directly that only that day, very memorable everywhere for the use of police dogs, electric cattle prods, and high-pressured fire-hoses on young men and women Negro demonstrators down South, those of them so 'liberal' in Princeton had gathered together and wired a righteously indignant message to President Kennedy in Washington to please do something to save the good name of the United States.

Another dinner, an official return affair for the group, was graced by Mr Albert Parvin himself. Flying in all the way from California, there was our benefactor in real flesh and blood, no longer some remote ghost donor like those foundations and trusts but remaining for us an unshakeable legend. An American of straight Armenian stock, he moved in a sprightly way among us in his silk suit in Princeton's famous Lowrie House, and he was full of high hopes that each of us there was at last well prepared, certified and properly diplomaed to return home and spread the good American word abroad.

In between times, the Colonel took the group out sight-seeing in New York City. In the course of it we watched the Stock Exchange in action, a real market of an affair except that it was all men and no women and wares, and we also, as the highlight of the day made the ascension of the Empire State Building, the most impressive address in all America, as the ad runs. Sandwiched between those engagements was a lunch date we had at Princeton House with a Vice-President of the Esso cartel, a proud Princetonian. Answering hushed queries as we ate, he summarily dismissed all talks about the existence of monopolies and of their ever ganging up against governments of countries in which they operate. Rather, he preferred to dwell on the huge benefits and blessings that accrue to the natives from Persia to Peru in the form of house

projects and other such vital amenities that they could never
have had were things left in the ineffectual, grabbing hands of
their puppet dictators. And returning to home grounds, he
spoke of how corporations like his are really the trust of the
people, operating only and solely in the interest and welfare
of the general public. Listening to him, I had some idea of
how a famous Senator, now dead, must have sounded atop
Capitol Hill as he grandly declared that there could never be
any conflict of interest in his promoting in Congress the cause
of an oil holding of which he happened to be the proud
possessor.

My other final engagement was with an old friend and
expert from the State Department in Washington. I think he
too was an old Princetonian, although his mission that day
had a more serious purpose than just social. It was to ascertain
from participants themselves whether or not they had found
the Parvin programme a useful experience. And to this end he
fed me at my interview with him with questions like these:
So did I think an examination at the end of the course would
be the one way of finding out who had gained from it? But
that wouldn't be fair, would it, with members of a group as
different in background and outlook as are your General and
that young prisons chap from your own country? And there is
the difficulty of language, as with the man from South
Korea. But isn't the real difficulty the fact that Princeton has
not all the faculties to meet the needs of a group like this?
For example, it has no School of Journalism like Columbia,
not that those of you who are journalists, a majority in the
group, really need any other training. But the agriculturist in
the group has had to go to Rutgers, away in New Brunswick
hasn't he? And coming to you personally, do you put politics
to use in the course of your creative writing? I never felt so
prompted in all my life.

One last concrete thing I clutched at was the idea of paying
my way on that very round-trip tour of the United States
that the Colonel and his governing colleagues at Princeton

were so determined on denying me. This the Greyhound Bus
people assured and guaranteed me for a ticket as low as $99.
So out I whipped those Esso sectional maps of America
already packed away in the heavy luggage I had long made
secure for its sea voyage home. With help and advice from
friends, in place of the Colonel, retired now for ever as far as
I was concerned, I mapped a route down South through
Washington to Houston in Texas and New Orleans in the
brothers Long's Louisiana; on from there (if I was still alive
and sound of limb after the colour barriers and bombs of
places like Birmingham!) past the deserts and sprawls of New
Mexico, and Arizona to the Grand Canyons of Colorado,
sheer as the Niagara Falls that I had already seen, and so to
Chicago on the Great Lakes, striking West from there on the
Golden Route to California and the Orient beyond.

From each of these places I made up my mind I would send
affectionate postcards to the Colonel and his wife. That,
someone said, should be real cute, although he wondered if
the recipients would not consider it so cheeky that they might
continue with their apparent pursuit of me out of the United
States. But tempting as the whole prospect undoubtedly was,
I told myself it was after all not really worth the trouble. New
York and Washington DC formed for me the great lounge
and hall of the American mansion with Princeton as the holy
recess and study. After being received and fêted and then
eventually shown the door, it would be superfluous of me, if
not exactly prowling and loitering, to insist on seeing the
walks and gardens that owners of the house call places like
California, the kitchen and incinerator that are spots like
Chicago and Pittsburgh, and the water-closet and cellars that
go by the name of the Deep South. So why not return home,
which is where no one rejects you, and perhaps make a few
stopovers in England and Europe, instead of using up time
and money, which was running out anyway, in hanging around
hosts now turned hostile?

And so it was one Wednesday night in May I found

myself on the midnight flight from New York's Idlewild Airport (as it was then) to London.

'Oh, do come back soon, JP!' Ruth and Sam, Cat and Israel, real Americans who had taken me in and would not let me go, all called out to me. But I was past the Customs barrier now, and all I could mumble back was: 'Yes, I do hope so!'